Primed

Primed

The Everyday Art of Rhetoric

Rachel Wei

NEW DEGREE PRESS

PRIMED

The Everyday Art of Rhetoric

ISBN   978-1-63676-830-4 *Paperback*

         978-1-63730-212-5 *Kindle Ebook*

         978-1-63730-274-3 *Ebook*

To my mother, Tsung-I, who has dedicated her
life to loving and supporting our family

And who tolerates my constant
attempts to pick apart language.

Contents

———

"Language is the blood of the soul into which thoughts run and out of which they grow."

—OLIVER WENDELL HOLMES JR.

Introduction

———

"It's not about what you say, it's how you say it." This might sound vaguely familiar, like a companion phrase of the often proffered "It's not what you know, it's who you know." Both sayings suggest that strong content should not be prioritized over other avenues of achieving your goals. As someone who considers being called a "nerd" a compliment, I have a natural aversion to this notion of sticking content in the backseat. Perhaps you feel similarly and are perplexed by how someone could persuade others with "just" words, regardless of if they made sense. Doesn't content matter more, and acquiring it deserve most of our energy? Furthermore, doesn't solid content undoubtedly prove our point for us? But, over the years, through my personal observations of professionals in a variety of fields, I've realized that having the ability to intentionally shape language to persuasively promote your wishes is not just a nice "bonus" skill to have, but essential for success.

I wanted to investigate how careful attention to rhetoric (which, in a nutshell, is "the art of speaking or writing effectively") benefits professionals in all fields, beyond those you'd expect rhetoric to be a cornerstone of, such as law or politics.

What would happen if immunology researchers could add skilled rhetorical communication skills to their impressive toolbox, which already includes knowing how to conduct immunoassays, make custom antibodies, and knock out individual genes of interest? Would becoming a "master rhetorician" help researchers secure additional grants that lead to the development of powerful, individually tailored cancer killing drugs?

Or, how would we, as everyday people, stand to benefit from being enlightened of the many ways rhetoric affects our lives whether we notice it or not? Better yet, what doors would open if we, too, gained mastery over this powerful tool and used it to accomplish our goals? What I discovered is that highly accomplished individuals in fields ranging from medicine to law to academia to business all understand how to wield the power of words to influence others, which ultimately helps them excel in their personal and professional lives.

With everyone from CEOs to politicians to parents pushing for children to pursue STEM careers, the humanities and arts have been sacrificed, deemphasized, and defunded.[1] The financial benefits of encouraging students to major in engineering or computer science, where fresh college graduates earn an average of $61,744 a year may seem obvious, especially when compared to the average starting salary of $45,032 a year for social science students (who are in disciplines typically considered under the "umbrella" of the humanities and

---

1 Alexandra Ossola, "Is the U.S. Focusing Too Much on STEM?," *The Atlantic*, December 3, 2014; Patricia Cohen, "A Rising Call to Promote STEM Education and Cut Liberal Arts Funding," *The New York Times*, February 21, 2016.

arts[2]). Perhaps you too are of the opinion that students have nothing to lose, and everything to gain, by opting out of an additional humanities course in favor of further bolstering their understanding of multivariable calculus.

Growing up in the age of tech and this "STEM as the future" obsession, I've often pondered that question and understand why many people grapple with it too. These STEM policies tell students that focusing on their "soft skills" simply isn't worth it. Why not spend more time and effort acquiring skills that correlate with and likely cause an increase in salary and therefore material well-being?

Educational stakeholders' emphasis on the financial rewards of those in STEM suggests that the additional benefit of taking another humanities class simply does not outweigh the costs (to their future salary, social status, bragging rights, etc.). Policymakers, parents, and sometimes teachers convince students that the costs of focusing on humanities courses are numerous, including sacrificing "a stable well-paying job," having to read dozens if not hundreds of pages each night, and enduring the quizzical eye of a professor always asking, *Well, I don't know. What do you think the author means?* Although rhetoric transcends all disciplines, students are often exposed to it in humanities courses, such as English classes. The trend towards putting STEM courses on a pedestal has helped lead to a diminished emphasis on communication skills, including rhetoric.[3]

2   David Deming, "In the Salary Race, Engineers Sprint but English Majors Endure," *The New York Times*, September 20, 2019.

3   Jo Handelsman and Megan Smith, "STEM for All," *National Archives and Records Administration*, February 11, 2016.

My examination of various research studies and successful professionals' career journeys reveal that far from deserving to be pushed into a corner, the humanities should be brought into the spotlight. Strong rhetorical and communication skills, rather than memorizing the periodic table or simply being "smart," are the key to success in all fields. After all, if you can't effectively express *why* your experiment should be supported, or *how* your findings are groundbreaking, you're likely not going to excel in STEM fields anyhow.

On top of this educational devaluing, many people don't consider having a solid grasp on rhetoric and language to be a high priority in their day to day lives. If anything, people seem to expect that the high-quality content of their papers, speeches, and articles will be enough. Oftentimes, professionals consider editing, where one ponders specific word choice, phrasing, grammar, and whether what they've written generally makes sense, to be of secondary importance. Some even think that the ability to present engaging presentations, yet another often scoffed at "soft" skill, isn't really necessary to convince the public that a recent scientific finding is revolutionary. After all, they think the content says it all. Others rely heavily on their educational and/or professional expertise in a field to bolster the legitimacy and reach of papers and speeches crafted with minimal attention to rhetoric. Many also think a high-level understanding of rhetoric can simply be "left to the professionals."

The problem with these views is that being aware of how language influences yourself and others, and then looking to master language is the key to effective persuasion. Learning to be persuasive in various situations is paramount, because most of our personal and professional success depends on our ability to convince others to agree with us, and subsequently take steps that will benefit us. Whether it's trying to convince your two-year-old that it is bedtime or cajole your boss into giving you a long-deserved raise, we cannot escape this need to convey our wishes to others in a way that inspires favorable action.

I felt compelled to delve deeper into this topic and share my findings with you because of the tremendous power and impact becoming aware of and learning to wield rhetoric can have on your life. From using effective rhetoric to help patients take meaningful actions towards living a healthier life, to being aware of how others use rhetoric to snag your vote, knowing that people are constantly using rhetoric to influence *you* is an important first step.

When I was younger, I didn't quite understand or process the way other peoples' rhetoric influenced my thoughts, including everything from who is the best pop singer of all time, to why *Harry Potter* should be considered a "classic" and allowed on the AP Language exam. However, the Trump Administration demonstrated the powerful effect rhetoric can have in a way that heightened many people's sensitivity to language. Because President Trump's rhetorical style was more direct and unfiltered than many of his predecessors, I was surprised to see how many individuals had a hard time differentiating between pure rhetoric and whether there was factual substance behind his claims.

Whether it was being stubbornly convinced that an event happened "because Trump said so" or that a country was "objectively bad" because of the president's remarks, I was stunned by how convinced people were that President Trump had valid evidence backing up his claims, even in the face of expert testimonies that invalidated his statements and the rigorous efforts of fact-checkers.[4] His rhetoric was so effective, it outweighed the influence of facts unearthed by these fact-checkers; many of his supporters didn't recognize the common rhetorical tools he used to make many of his claims *seem* substantive. This is not to say that using rhetorical tools is unethical or wrong; we all use them. However, watching President Trump hoodwink so many people helped kickstart my musings about the power of rhetoric and its ability to influence others, particularly those who are unaware that it's being used.

Whether you're an established professional looking to take your work to the next level and land a corner office, a high school or college student looking to leverage language to land internships and jobs, or someone who is seeking to convince friends and family members that *Breaking Bad* is without a doubt the best TV show of all time, this book is for you. You'll discover the history of rhetoric, key strategies and tools that people use on you, and how you can learn to wield them too. In this book, we'll analyze various success stories where using skilled rhetoric played a critical role in helping individuals achieve their goals. This guide will help "prime" you for success by teaching you how to recognize and respond to rhetoric in every aspect of your life.

---

4   Glenn Kessler and Joe Fox, "Analysis | The False Claims That Trump Keeps Repeating," *The Washington Post,* November 6, 2020.

Chapter 1

What is Rhetoric?

———

From spending hours each day tackling the emails in your inbox, to communicating who's in charge of dinner tonight, to typing up a highly anticipated brief for your boss, we all spend a significant portion of our waking hours communicating with each other. Regardless of whether we like it or not, successfully conveying our wishes, ideas, and complaints is an inherent part of our everyday lives. Despite the tremendous amount of time we have to spend communicating, we often don't give the topic of rhetoric the attention it deserves.

As with any other skill, mastering the art of rhetoric takes time, effort, and practice. It also takes an awareness of what rhetoric is and how, exactly, it plays a critical role in our lives. Throughout this book, we'll investigate how rhetoric differs in various professional fields and how the tips and tricks employed by successful professionals are ones we can incorporate into our everyday lives as well. But, for now, let's start out with a definition: rhetoric, as Merriam-Webster defines the term, is "the art of speaking or writing effectively."[5]

---

5   *Merriam-Webster*, s.v. "rhetoric (*n.*)," accessed November 1, 2020.

While it may sound a bit extravagant to describe rhetoric as an "art," when wielded with understanding and skill to achieve the need of a moment, rhetoric can be as powerful of a tool as a paintbrush in the hands of Van Gogh. Let's get into a brief history of rhetoric, and how this art form was created. Understanding the history behind rhetoric will be helpful in our journey to better understand what it is, and why it's still relevant today.

Any book on rhetoric wouldn't feel right without taking a brief detour to Ancient Greece, where the famous polymath intellectual, Aristotle, first coined the term. While Aristotle is known for his many contributions to Western thought, including his dedicated research in botany, metaphysics, and logic, his treatise on *The Art of Rhetoric* is one of his most famous accomplishments.

Born to the King of Macedonia Amyntas III in 384 BCE, Aristotle had access to the era's most highly influential teachers. He famously studied under Plato in Athens, and eventually opened his own school, or as they called it, academy, Lyceum. He was later hired to be Alexander the Great's personal tutor. With his highly academic background, Aristotle probably couldn't help but invent and expand on a few key areas of thought. But, as the focus of this book is on rhetoric, let's zero in on how Aristotle created the term "rhetoric" and what he meant by it.[6]

I should first clarify that I'm attributing Aristotle with creating the Aristotelian form of rhetoric. As we will explore

---

6   *Encyclopaedia Britannica Online*, Academic ed., s.v. "Rhetoric," accessed November 1, 2020.

throughout this book, there are endless types of rhetoric, and ways to effectively communicate. But, for the purposes of this work, I will be using Aristotelian rhetoric as my reference point. While I'm focusing on the history of Aristotelian rhetoric as the foundation of our exploration, I want to acknowledge that it isn't the only form out there. In fact, Aristotle's mentor Plato credits scholars in the city of Syracuse for developing the first formal teachings on rhetoric.

In the 5th century BCE, returning exiles had to use a new democratic legal system to reclaim their land in Syracuse. Much like the legal system in the United States and elsewhere, litigants depended on their ability to persuade in order to win cases. Teachers in the area capitalized on this new need, creating schools that offered courses on rhetoric, which was a new discipline at the time. Several years later, Aristotle sought to elevate the teachings of rhetoric by arguing that the process of learning to master rhetoric is an art. Considering rhetoric "an art of doing," and not merely "an art of making," Aristotle differentiated it from the sciences which he also studied.[7]

Aristotle argued that rhetoric is not concerned with "demonstrable matters," like physics or biology, where the truth is relatively objective once it's been proven. For example, if several well-designed and well-conducted scientific studies determine that drinking beverages with caffeine before bedtime decreases one's ability to sleep, there isn't much left to debate; an objective truth has been established or "demonstrated."[8]

---

7   Ibid.
8   Ibid.

On the other hand, rhetoric is concerned with "probable matters," which are much more subjective and hence, debatable. A probable matter you've debated could include anything from "Is a hotdog a sandwich?" to "Obviously, *Hamilton* is the best musical of all time." Because it is nearly impossible to prove "the truth" of probable matters, rhetoric can be harnessed to determine a variety of "inroads to truth." In other words, rhetoric is a powerful tool that can be used to shape (and possibly misconstrue) a subjective truth for an audience.[9]

To bring this a bit closer to home, picture what a child does when they really want something. Maybe it is the latest sneakers, a *Lord of the Rings* Lego set, or tickets to their favorite pop singer's concert. Whatever the item of interest is, children often attempt to persuade their parents that they really need an item with tactics such as, "But mom, I do really *need* a Nerf gun because my best friend Evan has one too!" Sometimes, children use the nuclear option, which is something along the lines of, "If you don't buy me a Nerf gun, it means you don't love me!"

These two examples, while they may sound childish, contain the basic elements of rhetoric that Aristotle defined in his writings: ethos, pathos, and logos. While most children likely don't use these three tenets of rhetoric intentionally, they often surface in conversations regardless and have an impact on their audience.

The first comment about a "need" for a Nerf gun shows a child, who we'll call Aiysha, using "logos" to persuade her

---

9   Ibid.

mom. Aiysha references her friend Evan, who we'll assume is someone her mom knows, to prove how a Nerf gun is clearly a reasonable request. After all, he's probably a friend who shares a lot in common with Aiysha's family. Maybe he has a similar socioeconomic situation, his parents are colleagues with her parents, or he lives in the same neighborhood. By pointing out the simple fact that Evan's parents bought him a Nerf gun, Aiysha is suggesting that the item is something reasonable, financially attainable, and even essential for her to have as well. Employing "logos" involves basing one's argument on logic and reason, which often includes harnessing analogies, examples, and even research to support your claim.[10]

The second nuclear option is an example of Aiysha using "pathos" to guilt her mom into getting her what she wants. Because "pathos" centers on stirring up someone else's emotions, it's often viewed as the least respectable rhetorical technique.[11] Emotions are often irrational and somewhat unreliable, but they're an avenue of persuasion, and thus rhetoric, nonetheless. It's extremely effective in fields such as advertising, that rely on pointing out our desires and insecurities to get us to act (i.e., buy whatever they're selling). In our second example, Aiysha is appealing to her mom's deep love for her in order to get what she wants. After all, what parent can bear being accused of not loving her/his child?

"Ethos" is the third and final type of persuasive appeal Aristotle defines. Ethos is often used by experts to assert that

10   TED, "Camille Langston: How to use rhetoric to get what you want," September, 2016, video, 2:35.

11   TED, "Camille Langston: How to use rhetoric to get what you want," 3:32.

their various academic and professional qualifications in and of themselves are plenty reason enough for you to trust them. They might name drop their alma mater or remind you that they spent eight years getting a PhD in the subject matter at hand to emphasize their credibility.[12] But, you don't have to really be an expert to use the ethos card. In addition to her logos- and pathos-based arguments, Aiysha might incorporate her expertise on Nerf guns, built on hours of dedicated research to prove how her claim of "needing" it is entirely credible and founded upon concrete data. She might list the top ten benefits of a Nerf gun and reference the safety features it has that makes accidents a nearly negligible risk.

We'll spend the rest of this book delving deeper into the nuances of rhetoric and how professionals make use of ethos, pathos, and logos. These terms may feel elementary but we will reference them and origins of Aristotelian rhetoric throughout this book as they form the foundations of rhetoric.

Mastering how to use language to persuade others is paramount to success. Whether it's convincing your boss to give you that hard-earned promotion or knowing how to coax your mom to incorporate senior friendly home features, rhetoric permeates through every aspect of our lives. Aristotle knew this and insisted that anyone can learn the art of rhetoric. He made a point to say rhetoric shouldn't be a tool that belongs to academics alone, but to all.

Aristotle observed that most of what we discuss in our everyday lives are probable matters. As such, the speaker often has

---

12   *TED*, "Camille Langston: How to use rhetoric to get what you want," 1:51.

an uncanny level of power to shape the minds and opinions of her or his audience. And, in probable matters, the speaker has almost complete power to decide which interpretation to assert as "the truth." In fact, Aristotle goes as far to say that oftentimes the content of what one says is not even really that important. Rather, one's ability to frame content persuasively in any situation is the key.[13]

Regardless of your profession or goal in life, taking the time to learn how to persuade others more effectively is invaluable. Knowing how to present the most favorable form of "the truth" is next level, and a powerful skill to have in your toolkit. Now that we've got our basics down, let's take a deeper look at how, on a practical level, renowned Ancient Roman orators thought about, practiced, and taught this art.

---

13   Christof Rapp, "Aristotle's Rhetoric," *Stanford Encyclopedia of Philosophy*, February 1, 2010.

Chapter 2

Stepping into the Past

———

*How Rhetoric Used to be
Taught in Ancient Rome*

We've established that rhetoric is an "art," but being an artist usually implies having some innate talent in a certain medium. Yet, Aristotle insisted that *anyone* can master language. Given that strong assertion, we might expect that the first teachers of rhetoric had some tricks up their sleeves, perhaps a foolproof way for all students to become better speakers. Luckily for us, some of the most accomplished ancient orators did in fact have some simple, rhetorical "formulas" we can begin with, and as prolific writers, they wrote all of their secrets down. Let's fast forward to Ancient Rome and see what some of its most skilled orators had to say.

Although the foundations of Aristotelian rhetoric were established in the fourth century BCE, famous Roman orators were instrumental in using their decades of practical political experience to shape how rhetoric should be taught.

As politicians, these orators spent most of their time speaking before crowds and crafting speeches, often on behalf of emperors. One such famous orator is Marcus Tullius Cicero. Born in 106 BCE, Cicero was a skilled lawyer, politician, and philosopher. Building upon Aristotle's idea that a true master of rhetoric should be persuasive in any situation, Cicero believed that a "perfect" orator had to have a broad range of knowledge in order to speak not only eloquently but substantively on whatever topic is at hand.[14]

Here, Cicero's beliefs differ from Aristotle's. While Aristotle argued that achieving a solid understanding of rhetoric is more than half the battle, Cicero posited that while knowing how to craft language is important, without solid content such maneuvering will only get you so far. Learning how to balance the need to painstakingly refine your rhetoric, while allocating enough time to make sure your basic content is sound, is something we'll hear various professionals provide their thoughts on later.

Incorporating Cicero's differing opinions on the topic, we now know that in order to be a skilled rhetorician, it's important to conduct research on your topic and, if possible, acquire background information on your audience. But, focusing on developing persuasive rhetoric should also be at the top of your list.

Now that we've had a brief introduction to Cicero's key beliefs regarding rhetoric, let's run through his "Five Canons of

---

14   Lumen Learning, "Principles of Public Speaking," The Roman Republic's Adoption of Rhetoric | Principles of Public Speaking, accessed February 23, 2021.

Rhetoric." These tenets are drawn from Cicero's handbook on oration, *De Inventione*, where his mature ideas and wisdom, despite being only around twenty years old, shine through as he suggests a methodical approach to becoming a better speaker. Cicero believed that "from eloquence those who have acquired it obtain glory and honour and high esteem" and that learning how to be eloquent "is not brought about by nature alone nor by practice, but is also acquired from some systematic instruction."[15]

According to Cicero, achieving skilled rhetoric requires five steps: invention, arrangement, expression, memory, and delivery. While Cicero focused on the art of oratory delivery, his teachings can be applied to other forms of rhetoric, including written rhetoric. We'll use his five-step framework as our jumping board because it summarizes what Cicero believed were the essentials to becoming a better speaker.

Invention

The first canon is "invention," which Cicero described as "the discovery of valid or seemingly valid arguments to render one's cause plausible."[16] In this step, speakers solidify what they want to persuade their audience of and what arguments they're going to use to do so.

This can involve forming a table of contents that clearly defines what you want to address in your speech. As someone

---

15　"The Five Canons of Rhetoric," *University of Arkansas Sam M. Walton College of Business*, accessed November 1, 2020.

16　Cicero, "De Inventione," *Loeb Classical Library*, 19.

who strongly believed in the merits of intellectual learning, particularly its ability to arm rhetoricians with the breadth and depth of knowledge needed to properly argue about any topic, Cicero insisted that knowing what you're trying to tackle is paramount to crafting a good argument. He believed outlining where you're headed enables you to pay attention to topics you might need a refresher on before sketching out any of your arguments.

Planning ahead also gives speakers the opportunity to determine what, exactly, they want and need to say. As many of us have experienced, simply knowing what you want to say doesn't guarantee that what actually comes out of your mouth is what you intended. Moreover, taking the time to carefully choose which arguments best prove their point saves orators a lot of time down the road. Because skilled orators pinpoint their end goal in advance, they can plan *how* to effectively get there well before the debate starts.

Arrangement

Next, we have the idea of "arrangement." Once you have your main talking points clearly listed, the next topic of concern is how you want to order them. As we'll see in other chapters, oftentimes how you present your ideas is as important as the content itself. So, pondering what the most strategic and persuasive way to organize your argument is far from a waste of time. Think about it this way: if you get all of this intentional thinking about research, content organization, and word choice out of the way first, you'll have a clearer idea of how your argument should be structured; you'll escape the headache of having to re-edit polished content because you realized it didn't quite fit in where you'd placed it.

For instance, if you're a CFO, presenting data and figures on how the company is doing this quarter to the board and major stockholders, you'd be pretty desperate to pass off even a disappointing quarter as "not that bad." In order to pull off this impression using objective numbers you can't ethically manipulate, one of the only and most effective options you have is to change the way you present the information. Depending on your audiences' personalities, which you discover through experience and/or preliminary research, you might choose to start the presentation off with something like this:

It's no secret that we have struggled this quarter. But this is a temporary loss, and we can expect high returns next quarter.

On the other hand, if you have a more pessimistic set of board members who react negatively to any sort of bad news, you might choose to kick things off a little differently:

I'd just like to say that our annual conference was a hit. We brought in 1.5x the profits we thought we would, and attendance was up twofold from last year.

While you'll be obligated to present the bad news about the quarter's overall low earnings later in the presentation, with some simple rearrangement you can set two entirely different moods.

Expression

Next, Cicero cites "expression" as his third tenet. By "expression," Cicero is referring to the often long-winded process of coming up with what you're actually going to say, down to the last word. Armed with knowledge and preparation from previous stages regarding where you want to go with your argument, it's finally time to put pen to paper. This phase includes various re-writes, edits, and crumpled up pieces of paper (or deleted word documents) that finally culminate into your final draft. This is also where a skilled rhetorician wouldn't shy away from spending a few extra hours. Going over possible synonyms, whether to use passive versus active voice, and even throwing in a suitable joke or two can go a long way in making your audience more receptive to your message.

Memory

Once you're happy with your content, it's time to move onto "memory." This is the tenet that is more applicable to oratory rhetoric than written rhetoric. While we may not have to memorize much of our material these days, Cicero couldn't hide behind a podium, computer, or slides when he gave a speech. Sometimes, even if you have the option to hide in a corner and read off a script, it can be advantageous to own the stage and give the audience the chance to see your full body language, feel your confident aura, and be blown away.

If you've ever had a music or dance recital, you'll know that achieving full memorization of a piece frees you up to focus on the tiny details and nuances that really bring a performance to life. Likewise, the advantage of memorizing a speech is to make sure you have the basics down so you can focus on using varying intonation to highlight the most striking facts in your speech, emphasizing an important point with a hand gesture, or walking around thoughtfully during moments of dramatic silence.

Delivery

Now that you have the content down, it's time to focus on the final stage: "delivery." This is when, having solidified your carefully crafted language, you can work on incorporating nonverbal cues that will make your speech even more persuasive and effective. "Delivery is the control of voice and body in a manner suitable to the dignity of the subject matter and the style," Cicero wrote.[17]

Whether it's making sure your hand gestures look intentional instead of awkward, finding the right places to insert impactful pauses, or walking around with a book on your head to refine your posture, delivery is what Aristotle would consider to be one of the most important parts of your preparation. Cicero's rhetorical framework takes some time and effort to learn, but it's a useful model to begin with.

Marcus Fabius Quintilianus added yet another layer to these tenets of being a skilled rhetorician. Born in northern Spain around a hundred years after Cicero in 35 CE, Quintilian, as he was more commonly known, was the first teacher to

---

17   Cicero, "De Inventione," *Loeb Classical Library*, 13.

receive a state salary teaching rhetoric and was later recruited by the Emperor Domitian to train his heirs.[18] Quintilian argued that people's speaking reflected not only their rhetorical skill but morality. Besides advocating for a return to more traditional forms of rhetoric, including Cicero's five canons, Quintilian taught that "the perfect orator" must not only be an effective speaker but a good person.

Quintilian encouraged a return to earlier, "pure" forms of rhetoric that didn't focus on embellishing speeches and writings for the sake of it, but to genuinely crafting a more precise and persuasive argument. Some of Quintilian's distaste for mere rhetorical "tricks" came from his experience arguing in courts. [19] Quintilian saw firsthand how distracting and short-lived embellishments were in the greater scheme of winning a legal argument and thought that such use of rhetorical tools was unnecessary and ineffective. Near the end of his life he wrote his famous *Institutio Oratoria,* which consists of twelve books on rhetoric and was heavily adapted by Renaissance scholars. "If our definition of rhetoric as the science of speaking well implies that an orator must be a good man, there can be no doubt about its usefulness," Quintilian wrote. Regarding speech, Quintilian described it as "that in which mankind excels all other living things" and insists that "there is no art which yields a more grateful recompense for the labour bestowed upon it."[20]

---

18   Lumen Learning, "Principles of Public Speaking," The Roman Republic's Adoption of Rhetoric | Principles of Public Speaking, accessed February 23, 2021; Martin Lowther Clarke, "Quintilian," *Encyclopædia Britannica,* last updated January 1, 2021.

19   Ibid.

20   Quintilian, "Institutio Oratoria," Book 2, accessed February 10, 2021, 11, 17.

In Chapter 15, I spotlight how rhetoric, while a beautiful skill, can be used for evil. Quintilian believed that those who used rhetoric frivolously or who wielded it without upright character were not, no matter how skilled, true masters of rhetoric. In fact, Quintilian insisted that at its core, rhetoric is "the good man speaking well."[21]

---

21   Lumen Learning, "Principles of Public Speaking."

Chapter 3

The Here and Now

―――

How Rhetoric is Taught Today in the US

After hearing about the strong philosophical and academic origins of rhetoric, some of you may be wondering why no one has formally taught you rhetoric before. While most schools teach students about literature and how to write analytical essays, rhetoric is typically not referenced directly. Let's take a closer look at why that is, and how rhetoric can be taught in schools today.

An essential skill students learn from the time they can read is how to write. An invaluable method of communication, writing is often our first introduction to how language is shaped purposefully and how it can be analyzed with the author's intention in mind. Although schools often frame writing as a skill that can be easily learned and refined by the time you're out of high school, learning to master rhetoric takes a lifetime of practice. While some students breathe a huge sigh of relief when stalking out of their last college writing course, most adults realize that the idea of being done with writing "forever" after finishing your formal education is nothing more than a pipe dream.

Marvin Diogenes is the longstanding Director of Stanford's Program in Writing and Rhetoric and the Associate Vice Provost for Undergraduate Education. He studied English as an undergraduate at Stanford University and refined his craft with a Masters of Fine Arts (MFA) in Creative Writing from the University of Arizona. It was during Diogenes' time in Arizona that he learned how to create university writing courses, with a special emphasis on teaching with a rhetorical lens. Returning to Stanford in 2000 to help revive its undergraduate writing program, Diogenes has spent his career trying to teach students not merely how to write but to become masters of rhetoric.

When I spoke with him, Diogenes reflected on how many students come into Stanford pretty confident that they're "good writers." First-year college students can be a bit arrogant, still bristling with pride that they wrote a college application essay that landed them at a top US educational institution. This arrogance isn't merely due to students' personal pride, but what they've been taught about writing, i.e., that it's a skill that's easily mastered once and for all.

Diogenes emphasized how he tries to teach students that rhetoric is an art, which goes beyond being able to form coherent sentences. However, most students aren't receptive to the idea that it'll take them a lifetime to master rhetoric, so Diogenes devotes substantial course time to challenging students' ingrained views of writing and rhetoric as elementary skills not worth a significant time investment.

Growing up, I was also fed this idea that writing is a skill that one not only could but should master with a limited amount of practice. If students were still struggling with how to organize their essays (which we learned from Cicero is more important than it might seem) by their junior year, they were given the impression that they were behind and weren't "natural writers." This view is not only discouraging but inaccurate as being an effective writer is something that comes with time and guidance that should extend beyond one's formative years at school.

Rather than try to teach sleep-deprived high schoolers the nuances of language and all its potential, my teachers decided it'd be easier to teach writing as a series of outlines. We received one outline for historical essays, another for literature, and yet another for how to analyze the US government. Though intended to provide students with a helpful "cheat sheet" as to what "good writing" looked like, teaching writing as a series of outlines rather than the process of how to put thought on paper created a reliance on writing "formulas." These rules dictated everything from the order an essay should be written in, to how many quotes were "appropriate" for one paragraph and quenched students' individual writing voice in favor of a dry, more formal tone.

I've had many peers complain that teachers' writing expectations could differ widely, which they found extremely confusing and discouraging. Although they had learned a previous teacher's "writing style" (i.e., essay formula), they were now struggling to adapt this structure to fit another teacher's expectations. In other words, they were realizing that they didn't actually know how to write. This understandably caused students to panic as they were often given a maximum of four essay assignments a semester and couldn't afford to do poorly on any of them. For some, this fear of not knowing how to write for oneself drove them to plagiarize other people's work which led to serious academic consequences.

If my peers and I were taught that mastering writing involves not memorizing and adhering to one or even a hundred outlines but learning how to harness words to achieve your goal in any context, we would be better prepared for the many ways we're expected to write throughout our lives. As I grew older and encountered scientific writing, journalistic writing, creative writing, poetry, and so many other forms, I was a bit surprised at how the writing "formulas" teachers taught me didn't prepare me for the many ways I'd be expected to write in real life.

Similar to how memorizing the quadratic equation and understanding the basics of calculus doesn't enable one to solve real-world engineering problems, learning how to write through rote memorization and adherence to strict rules doesn't equip students to face the many, varied situations in which they will be expected to communicate effectively as adults.

Because many students are educated using this method all the way until (and sometimes through) college, Diogenes often finds that his greatest battle is getting students to change their mindset about writing and rhetoric. "You cannot rely on a predetermined skill set to communicate effectively," Diogenes said. "Rhetoric requires you to analyze the situation in which you're trying to communicate with attention to your audience."

The way Diogenes often describes rhetoric is as a triangle between the speaker, the audience, and the subject at hand. True masters of rhetoric need to be persuasive and effective communicators in any context, paying close attention to the interaction of these three key elements of a conversation. And, as with any subject, when students are taught formulaic shortcuts instead of how to develop and perfect their craft over time, they often struggle when different circumstances arise, and they have to apply what they've (supposedly) learned.

While we focused on Aristotelian rhetoric in our brief history overview, any unique way of communicating through language is a form of rhetoric in its own right and worth studying to further expand your understanding of rhetoric. At Stanford, Diogenes has been trying to incorporate different forms of rhetoric and diverse content into the program's courses. "You can't teach all forms of rhetoric or all cultural rhetorical traditions in one quarter, but you at least have to make students aware, especially given the diversity of the student population at Stanford," Diogenes said. "If the students walking in your classroom are coming from multiple rhetorical traditions, it is not only a disservice, but it is morally wrong to teach them one form of rhetoric as if it's the only form of rhetoric."

Diogenes reminds students that although Aristotelian rhetoric is typically the foundation of rhetorical teaching (at least in Western countries), it is not all encompassing. One exercise he likes is to ask students to write about their "home rhetoric" for ten minutes at the beginning of his workshop. "Home rhetoric" can be anything from the old-fashioned idioms only grandparents still use, to the vernacular of a certain language or culture that parents brought with them from their home countries. After students have had the chance to reflect on these various forms of rhetoric, Diogenes emphasizes that although they may not view the way their mom talks or grandparents' language as "rhetoric," it is unique and valuable.[22]

As we learned earlier, at its core, rhetoric is the art of communicating effectively and persuasively in all situations. Because there are infinite situations we can find ourselves in, there are endless ways we can use language to communicate. Oftentimes, the way we persuade others at home looks quite different from the way we communicate at work; that's perfectly acceptable. There are myriad forms of rhetoric, and that's why it's important to view it as an art and not a single skill.

Another key reason why it's critical to teach students from a young age that writing and rhetoric are not merely skills or tools to be learned once (or twice) but an art form that will forever remain applicable to their life, is that it allows them to develop a healthy understanding that skilled writing and thinking are interconnected. When students are taught that writing is a purely subjective tool they can use to express themselves as they see fit, it's easy to fall into the trap of being dismissive of one's critics. While rhetoric is a skill that

---

22 Although we will be focusing on the Aristotelian canons of rhetoric in this work, here are a few resources on cultural rhetoric that may be of interest: "Cultural Rhetoric," *Stanford Undergrad*, accessed February 10, 2021; Robert Shuter, "The Cultures of Rhetoric," *International and Intercultural Communication Annual*, 18, no. 22 (January 1999): 11-18.; Barry Brummett, *Rhetoric in popular culture* (Thousand Oaks: Sage Publications, 2017).

provides rhetoricians with substantial wiggle room to decide how to best communicate their message, students need to learn that regardless of which avenues they decide to use, they are still responsible for whether their message lands as they intend to. We'll discuss this further in our chapter on Law, but being humble enough to admit when the way you chose to use rhetoric isn't effective, instead of blaming your audience for "not getting it," is important. Teaching students to take ownership of their message, aiming to leave their audience with no other choice but to understand and be convinced of their point, will help prevent them from developing an allergic reaction to critical feedback that will ultimately prevent them from growing as a rhetorician.

Throughout my years in school I've heard, "Oh, she just doesn't like my writing style" countless times. While I sympathized with how disorienting it can be to encounter teachers with varied writing styles, I always felt that it was a shame that my peers were dismissing thoughtful critiques of their rhetorical abilities as a simple distaste for their "style." Diogenes mentioned how this pride and fear prevents people from developing a growth mindset that will enable them to become better writers and thus communicators, which is detrimental to their future prospects.

Although many of us may consider ourselves to be excellent communicators and thus skilled rhetoricians, I'd like you to think back to the last time you had to write. It could be an email to your boss, a cover letter for a job application, or a scholarly paper. Do you ever panic and feel a bit of fear rising in you as you stare at the cursor blinking on your blank screen? If you do, you're in good company. When adults are taught as students that they can "escape" writing, many will choose that road and lose out on their chance to take further courses (or be open to feedback) that will help them become more effective communicators. This attitude is problematic. As I'm sure you've experienced in your life, and as we'll explore in the coming chapters, effective communication is the backbone of most if not all essential functions of human life and society and a key skill for success.

Students will grow up to become adults who will have to effectively use rhetoric to make a compelling case for a promotion, teach their children why sharing is important, and explain to their colleagues their stance on controversial issues like universal healthcare. Teaching students that they can forget about rhetoric after completing school and neglecting to equip them with rhetorical essentials they can learn to master over a lifetime robs them of their ability to communicate effectively. And as a result, we're hindering them from being the best they can be. There's a saying that goes something like this: you may think you're done with writing, but writing is never done with you.

Chapter 4

It's Not Just the Facts that Matter

———

Rhetoric + Journalism

You're in an active war zone, hopping in army tanks with soldiers dressed in combat gear, clutching your recording equipment. Or you might be sitting in a TV studio trying to piece together a "breaking news" memo and forward it to your network abroad. On yet another day, you might be sleuthing through your industry sources, trying to convince someone to give you a tip on an unfolding scandal. While these descriptions filled with chaos, publicity, and detective work may sound far-fetched to some of us, it's part of every-day life for journalists.

Journalists work in an ever-changing world, which means they're always in a time crunch. As you may have experienced in your life, it's often in times of urgency that we're the most grateful for the time we spent perfecting our core skills. When we master something, it allows us to work more efficiently; it's easier to "get in the zone" and let your expertise take the lead.

For journalists, rhetoric is one of, if not their top core skill. Dealing with constant deadlines and uncertainty of what they're going to cover next, journalists who've been taught how to write and communicate effectively have a huge advantage over others. Having the opportunity to learn these skills and refine them under the tutelage of masters allows these journalists to be rhetorically strategic even under high-stress situations.

While journalists spend a fair amount of time getting together facts, quotes, and sound bites, assembling the raw material for an article is just the tip of the iceberg. Producing high-quality journalism is a time-consuming process that involves multiple rounds of edits, pondering how to approach a story, and how to best tell it. Having been an amateur journalist since high school, I've come to appreciate how much thought journalists put into crafting articles. Great journalism involves traveling domestically (and sometimes internationally), tracking down sources, months and even years of investigative work, and the ability to adapt as stories change and unfold. Being a successful journalist requires not only knowing what the story is but *how* to tell it.

After journalists have conducted the necessary research, they have to decide how to best tell the story at hand. This involves dedicating time to think through not only the facts and data they've gathered but how to weave them into a coherent and accurate retelling. On top of the stress of a twenty-four-seven news cycle, journalists also have strict editorial deadlines they have to meet. With such a tight timeline, it wouldn't be surprising if some people decided to cut corners, perhaps haphazardly stitching the facts loosely together and leaving it to the reader to connect the dots.

Of course, such an approach is not ideal, and oftentimes not the ethical course of action. So, what do journalists do to succeed in such a high-pressure environment? One strategy is to be more efficient and skilled than the competition. Oftentimes, journalists can't speed along the processes of data collection or convincing sources to go on the record. But something they can control is the latter part of the process: crafting the article.

As we've discussed, writing can involve a lot of head-scratching and sleepless nights making sure your language conveys what you intend. Because journalists don't have the time to follow Cicero's five canons of rhetoric on every story, having a solid grasp on rhetoric is imperative in helping journalists successfully complete their job in a timely manner.

Achieving the gold standard of releasing accurate, evidence based, digestible, unbiased information is essential because journalism has wide ranging effects on people's lives. Often called "the fourth branch" of government, journalists collectively act as a "watchdog" for the rich and powerful making sure they are held accountable to the public for their actions.[23] Journalists also provide everyday citizens with valuable information that helps them make informed,

---

23   Delbert Tran, "The Fourth Estate As The Final Check," *Yale Law School: Media Freedom and Information Access Clinic*, November 22, 2016.

strategic decisions, such as whether it's a good time to take out a loan or whether a certain pesticide is safe to use in their garden.

Tom Lee is Member-in-Charge of the Nashville branch of the law firm Frost Brown Todd. Although he is currently a successful attorney, Lee actually began his professional career as a journalist. After attending the University of Georgia for two years, he left to become a reporter covering local and state Tennessee government and politics. Subsequently, Lee received a BA in Journalism from the University of Tennessee, Knoxville, and headed to Vanderbilt Law School. Lee's work ethic and mindful storytelling as a journalist landed him roles in national award-winning documentaries and won him two regional Emmy Awards.

When I spoke with Lee about how he's learned to refine his rhetoric over the years, he credits his career in journalism for teaching him the valuable skill of clearly laying out the facts of a story in a concise yet engaging manner. Much like how lawyers harness rhetoric to make a compelling yet succinct case for their client in court, journalists often have limited space and time to tell important stories.

During the Persian Gulf War in 1990, Lee was sent overseas to cover a unit from Tennessee that was having a hard time adjusting to life at war. Because the Gulf War broke out suddenly, many soldiers had little time to mentally prepare for their deployment and were struggling to get along with their unit leadership as well. After speaking with various soldiers in the camp, Lee did his best to capture their stories and bring them back home to their fellow Tennesseans.

However, a few weeks after his story was published, Lee received a jarring letter. While Lee and other journalists are used to receiving mail of all sorts, including those filled with accusations and insults, he was taken aback by what this family had to say about his reporting.

The commander of the struggling Tennessean unit Lee had written about committed suicide a few weeks after Lee's article was published. His family was writing to tell Lee that they thought his article was partially to blame for their son's death. They accused him of framing soldiers' stories in a way that suggested their son was responsible for the unit's struggles. In other words, the family thought Lee's rhetoric contributed to their son's death.

Deeply moved and troubled, Lee frantically pored through his interview notes and transcripts, searching if he had indeed been careless in his writing and miscommunicated something. He was looking for indications of personal bias and whether he told the soldiers' stories fairly. In the end, Lee concluded that as tragic as the commander's death was, he had told as accurate and fair of a story as he could. However, after this incident he became critically aware of the constant power he had as a journalist to impact readers with his rhetoric. How he shaped and phrased his stories mattered and could be a matter of life or death to some. "I came away from that review confident that we had told the story people had told us," Lee said. "But I also came away from that experience literally aware of the impact that getting something wrong would cause."

After this incident, Lee was reminded that his rhetoric as a journalist is of the utmost importance. No matter what time crunch he was under, detailed decisions in word choice, which quotes to use, and how he portrayed people mattered. They had a real impact on readers' lives, and he couldn't afford to be careless.

Lee's experiences reveal how deeply our rhetoric can affect those around us. When we unleash our words out into the world, we are held accountable for its effects, positive or negative. If we're not skilled in evaluating our language, we risk harming others, even if we didn't intend to.

Staying vigilant against bias

Now that we've heard Tom Lee's story, and how much rhetorical power journalists have, it's not surprising how guarded some journalists can be against displaying any signs of bias. A lot of what journalists report, although not inherently controversial, are deemed so because they're controversial among readers. Once their work is released to the public, it's subject to endless analyses, including critics picking apart their work—and sometimes their character.

Something readers dislike finding is any hint of "bias" in journalists' work. Although it would do us well to remember that journalists are people too, and thus have personal opinions that sometimes unconsciously seep into their writing, many readers expect nothing less than perfection.

When people say they crave "fair" reporting, they're often referring to what they consider to be unbiased perspective. As writers, journalists have only their pen as their sword, so language is both their weapon and potential downfall. If journalists signal with their rhetoric that they lean towards one side or the other, they risk losing the trust of their readers. This fear drives many serious journalists to always keep an eye on their rhetoric and how their message is coming across to readers. They don't simply rely on their good intentions but work to make sure their writing can be mistaken for nothing other than high-quality, unbiased journalism.

Bob Woodward is a renowned investigative journalist who has worked for *The Washington Post* since 1971. He is currently an Associate Editor at the *Post*, has won two Pulitzer prizes, and written fourteen number one bestsellers about presidents ranging from Clinton to Obama to Trump. Perhaps most memorably, Woodward played a leading role in uncovering the Watergate scandal in 1972.[24] With his decades of journalistic experience, Woodward has learned to refine his rhetoric, particularly in regard to preserving an unbiased outlook in his reporting.

Working in Washington, DC, Woodward emphasizes the particular importance of not using any words that can be interpreted as politically biased in order to maintain trust. Since journalists depend on connections with sources to get much needed tips, insider information, and quotes, trust is essential to journalistic success. If journalists aren't trusted and respected, they have a hard time landing interviews with politicians and high-flying figures in the DC community. Woodward pinpoints how using rhetoric to convey one's neutrality is paramount to earning trust and respect in the field of Journalism.

---

24 "Bob Woodward," Bob Woodward, accessed Feburary 23, 2021.

Neutrality in action

Woodward and Carl Bernstein were *The Washington Post* reporters leading the charge to uncover what is now known as Nixon's Watergate scandal.[25] Details began leaking in 1972 and culminated with President Nixon resigning in 1974. As you can imagine, discovering that the current President of the United States is engaging in illegal campaign activities can seem surreal and exciting. However, it was especially during this unfolding that Woodward insisted no one in the newsroom even mention the word "impeachment." Even though everyone involved knew it would likely happen if Nixon didn't resign first, Woodward wanted to avoid this word to keep his image as an unbiased reporter clean and clear. "We can never use that word 'impeach,' 'impeachment' in the newsroom because people will think we're on a political crusade," Woodward said.[26]

So, even in the comfort of a familiar newsroom surrounded by colleagues, Woodward warns that it's still important to send a consistent message of one's neutrality at all times. This includes holding your tongue at dinner parties and personal events to avoid giving away your position on newsworthy issues. Word gets around easily, so if journalists are careless with their rhetoric even with close friends and family, that can spell trouble for their professional image as well. Similarly, in our everyday lives, it's important to have a keen awareness of what language we're using and what it may imply to others. A

---

25 History.com Editors, "Watergate Scandal," *History.com*, last updated September 25, 2019.

26 Bob Woodward, "Guiding Principles" in "Bob Woodward Teaches Investigative Journalism," November 13, 2020, MasterClass video, 4:08.

careless word can lead to a diminished professional reputation or even a career-ending scandal that one didn't intend.

Another way Woodward uses rhetoric to convince the public and politicians of his political neutrality is by making sure he contributes to different media networks. Because Fox News is widely considered a conservative network and CNN a liberal station, Woodward makes sure he appears on both. By doing so, he is communicating to the audience that he is someone who doesn't pick and choose sides. By appearing on networks across the media political spectrum, Woodward gained viewers' trust across the aisle.[27] This has allowed Woodward to conduct in-depth interviews with politicians like President Trump who are often distrustful of "mainstream" journalists. Building trust and rhetorically signaling neutrality in his professional and personal life has helped Woodward become a world-renowned journalist.

Woodward is no stranger to interviewing high profile individuals who are experts in dodging his straightforward questions. Politicians in particular often have a knack for evading questions and framing facts in their favor. But, whether sources want to talk or not, it's journalists' job to get the information out. Getting powerful people to answer questions they don't want to address is no easy task. Luckily, Woodward has some tried and true rhetorical tricks up his sleeve to make sure he and the public get the answers they deserve. In interviews, Woodward signals he is serious about getting answers to his questions through repetition. "By persisting with the same questions, we're saying to him we really

---

27   Bob Woodward, "Guiding Principles," 5:55.

want answers," Woodward said regarding interviewing then candidate Trump.[28]

Here, Woodward doesn't rely on sharp words or interjections that may offend candidate Trump. Doing so could risk an abrupt ending to the interview—a missed opportunity to draw out answers to controversial topics for the public and to give Trump a chance to tell things from his point of view. By simply using repetition, Woodward is able to nudge his reluctant interviewee to either answer the question or risk looking like he has something to hide from the public.

Oftentimes, the public relies on journalists to get concrete confirmations and denials of important issues. By refining and employing his rhetorical skills, Woodward has been able to serve the public for decades, probing politicians and other powerful figures for answers to issues concerning the public, while maintaining a respectful relationship with them that enables his work to continue.

Do journalists really have rhetorical bias?

Interestingly, as much as Woodward is careful to not portray any journalistic bias, a meta-analysis of fifty-nine studies found that there are "no significant biases" in the newspaper industry, including news magazines.[29] This may be

---

28 Bob Woodward, "Students Dig Into Woodward's Interview With Trump," 2:09.

29 Dave D'Alessio and Mike Allen, "Media Bias in Presidential Elections: A Meta-Analysis," *Journal of Communication* 50, no.4 (December 2000): Pages 133–156.

surprising as everyone from business leaders to politicians often accuse media outlets of being terribly biased. A 2020 Pew Research Center Poll found that while 70 percent of liberal Democrats trusted CNN, only 16 percent of conservative Republicans did.[30] On the other hand, while 75 percent of conservative Republicans trust Fox News, only 12 percent of liberal Democrats trust it. Although the meta-analysis found that "television network news showed small, measurable, but probably insubstantial coverage and statement biases," how is it that audience members have such a different take on outlets' supposed bias?

In his book titled *Balance and Bias in Journalism*, Guy Starkey, a professor of Radio and Journalism at the University of Sunderland, explores how messaging is always consciously or unconsciously shaped by journalists. Starkey mentions how deadlines and other journalistic constraints often heighten the amount of careless rhetoric used. Moreover, because media reporting relies on rhetoric to convey not only facts but interpretations of what the facts mean for readers, articles are inherently shaped not only by journalists but the audience.

When you read a book, your personal experiences, opinions, and biases color the story. That's why some people profess to love *Great Expectations*, declaring it the cream of the crop, while you may be struggling to get past page twenty and think it's the worst book ever written. "Every media representation is a construct, formed from elements chosen in whole or in part to offer those audiences insight into a

30   John Gramlich, "Q&A: How Pew Research Center Evaluated Americans' Trust in 30 News Sources," *Pew Research Center*, January 24, 2020.

'reality' in which they are supposedly interested," Starkey wrote. "It follows therefore, that the chances of these being wholly accurate representations are remote. Even if unintentional, representing 'reality' within the time and resource constraints upon all media can introduce distortions that obfuscate more than they illuminate."[31]

But it's important to remember that journalists don't bear the burden of interpretation alone. News reporting, while likely not as open to interpretation as a fictional novel, still leaves room for us to insert our own opinions into what we're reading.

Have you ever scanned a news article on what Congress is currently debating, saw a senator's name you recognized, and rolled your eyes before you even read that senator's quote? It's okay to admit it; we all react, sometimes viscerally, to people, places, and organizations that we think we know. Such natural reactions color our interpretation of the news. "Audiences interpret media output in ways that accommodate information in the text that is new to them within established frameworks of knowledge and understanding," Starkey wrote. "They will reference new information to prior knowledge, attitudes and expectations they have already developed either firsthand or through proxies."[32]

Now you probably have a better idea of why Woodward was almost paranoid about his rhetoric and how it can be interpreted. Trying to be as clear and neutral as possible is a sort of

---

31 Guy Starkey, *Balance and Bias in Journalism: Representation, Regulation and Democracy* (Basingstoke: Palgrave Macmillan, 2007), 1.

32 Guy Starkey, *Balance and Bias in Journalism: Representation, Regulation and Democracy*, 3.

self-protection for journalists. But what can we do, as consumers of the media, to protect ourselves from journalists' unconscious biases and our own? As we will discuss further in the chapter on politics, exposing yourself to multiple news sources is your best bet. This way, you'll be able to counter or at least balance out the effects of journalistic deadlines and any media leanings.

Let's take a look at a specific event and how various news outlets highlighted different aspects of it. Judge Amy Coney Barrett's confirmation was hotly contested. Democrats were upset that President Trump and Senate Republicans were trying to push through candidates weeks before the presidential election, particularly when Senate majority leader Mitch McConnell had advocated against confirming any candidates until after an upcoming presidential election.[33] On the other hand, President Trump and Republicans maintained that a President has the right to nominate and confirm a candidate before a term is officially up. However, Republicans held the opposing opinion when President Obama nominated Judge Merrick Garland to replace Justice Antonin Scalia after his sudden death in the Spring of 2016. Then, Senate majority leader Mitch McConnell stated that "the American people should have a say in the court's direction" to support his refusal to hold a Senate vote on Garland.[34]

With that context in mind, let's see how different news outlets highlighted different aspects of Barrett's confirmation. BBC, a media outlet based in England, highlighted several hot

---

33 Marianne LeVine, "McConnell Fends off Accusations of Hypocrisy over Holding Supreme Court Vote," *Politico,* September 22, 2020.

34 Ron Elving, "What Happened With Merrick Garland In 2016 And Why It Matters Now," *NPR,* June 29, 2018).

topic issues that Democrats questioned Barrett about. Subtitles in the article spotlighted climate change, abortion, and healthcare. The article also included many direct quotes that presented readers with Barrett's actual responses, leaving it up to them to form opinions about whether those responses were satisfactory or not.[35]

Fox News, trusted by many Republicans and conservative viewers, highlighted Barrett's clever use of rhetorical tools to avoid answering questions about the Affordable Care Act (ACA). While news outlets came out with multiple articles as the hearings continued, this article almost praised Barrett's use of pathos and storytelling to skirt Senator Cory Booker's question. "Senator, I could certainly empathize with people who are struggling," Barrett responded. "I could empathize with people who lack health care. You know, one of the things that was so striking to me when we went to get our daughter Vivian from the orphanage in Haiti was the lack of access to basic things like antibiotics."[36]

In this quote, we can see how Barrett uses her personal family experience to convey a sense of support for health care generally, without committing to supporting the ACA specifically (which was what Senator Booker was asking her to comment on). While Fox News viewed such rhetorical strategies as evidence of Barrett's suitability for the Supreme Court, other news outlets were not so admiring of Barrett's evasive techniques.

35 Anonymous, "Amy Coney Barrett: Trump US Supreme Court Pick Grilled on Presidential Powers," *BBC News*, October 15, 2020.

36 Marisa Schultz, "Judge Amy Coney Barrett Flips the Script on Democrats over Health Care, Notes When She Adopted Daughter," *Fox News*, October 13, 2020.

In contrast, *The New York Times* is considered a liberal leaning newspaper. In one article about Barrett's confirmation, *NYT* zeroed in on Barrett's evasive response to climate change: "I would not say I have firm views on it." Here, Barrett uses passive voice in "would not say" to distance herself from her own noncommittal views on climate change. Instead of stating, "I do not have firm views," Barrett almost responds in third person, as if she's commenting on someone else's views. Unlike the BBC and Fox News articles, the *NYT* article interviewed numerous academic experts, including scholars from New York University (NYU) Law School to weigh in on Barrett's rhetoric and support their interpretation of her rhetoric as intentionally evasive.[37]

Finally, let's take a look at CNN, which is considered a liberal news source. In an article on Barrett's confirmation, CNN focused not on what Barrett said (as the Fox News piece did), but what she *didn't* say. The article also compared and contrasted Barrett's responses to other conservative judges, such as Chief Justice John Roberts' responses during his Supreme Court confirmation hearing. The article also made some bold, pessimistic predictions right off the bat, arguing that "If Judge Amy Coney Barrett rules in the vein she testified before the Senate Judiciary Committee this week, Americans' personal privacy rights would be pushed back more than a half century."[38]

---

37 John Schwartz and Hiroko Tabuchi, "By Calling Climate Change 'Controversial,' Barrett Created Controversy," *The New York Times*, updated October 22, 2020.

38 Joan Biskupic, "Amy Coney Barrett's Answers Were Murky but Her Conservative Philosophy Is Clear," *CNN*, October 15, 2020.

From this brief analysis of what four different news outlets emphasized, we can see how they each focused on different aspects of the hearings, down to specific responses (or non-responses). They also painted Barrett's responses differently. Some framed her evasive answers as strategic and admirable, while others framed them as suspiciously evasive, even when compared to other judges. All this goes to say that while journalists do their best to be neutral and make a good faith effort to present us with unfiltered facts, rhetoric inevitably colors and frames events. Moreover, we, as readers, also see information through our individual lens and filters. So, it's important to be aware of journalists' rhetoric and our own biases. The more sources you read, the better you'll get at spotting differences in journalistic rhetoric which will help you become a savvier media consumer.

To sum up, rhetoric matters—a lot—in journalism. Because journalists' biases can color their articles, they have to be particularly wary of spotting and eliminating any biased rhetoric or framing of events before their work reaches the public. But we, as audience members, aren't completely innocent either. Whenever we absorb media, we are inevitably letting our own opinions, biases, and beliefs color what we're reading or watching. So, we should make an effort to observe our own reactions towards events, news channels, and people. Journalism is a two-way street, so if both journalists and readers can learn to pay more attention to our personal biases and rhetoric, we'll all be better off and able to more effectively absorb news with an open mind.

Chapter 5

Helping Doctors Save Lives

———

Rhetoric + Medicine

If I asked you how many times you've failed in your life, what would you say? Would you hesitate and shift uncomfortably in your seat? Or maybe you would counter my question with another and cleverly ask what my definition of "failure" is. Patients struggling with health challenges are often accused of "failing," which is demoralizing and doesn't help address their situation.

Imagine if a doctor asked a patient how many times they've "struggled" or what "shortcomings" they've had in their life instead. It sounds less accusatory, and conveys a sense of accepting, open-minded curiosity. I know I would have an easier time answering what I've struggled with, rather than being prompted to label a challenging time as a "failure." Although we know the effect swapping out one word for another can have, sometimes we're perplexed as to *why* we feel such a huge difference.

In previous chapters, we've laid the groundwork for why we should never underestimate the impact rhetoric can have on whoever is on the receiving end of our messages. As we've seen in our study of Judge Amy Coney Barrett's Senate confirmation hearing, "framing" can have a significant impact on how the same event is presented to an audience and provide guidance for how they should react. We'll delve deeper into this idea of "framing" in our chapter on politics. But it's also a powerful rhetorical tool in medicine because the way in which a situation or challenge is framed affects the likelihood that a patient chooses to accept and act on important medical advice.

Returning to the example we started this chapter with, labeling an event as a "failure" versus a "setback" can have a significant impact on how people respond to doctors' questions and how likely they are to seek solutions to their challenges. Flagging something as a failure can lead people to shame-induced avoidance instead of providing patients with the courage to face the obstacle at hand and seek help. Being wary of judgmental diagnostic rhetoric is imperative if doctors want to truly help their patients.

How would you feel if your doctor described your lack of faithfully exercising for at least thirty minutes every day as a "failure?" Perhaps you'd feel a bit discouraged or even defensive of your current lifestyle choices regardless of whether you think you need to get to the gym more or not. Such language could encourage you to think something along the lines of, *Well, you know what? I'm extremely busy. I don't have easy access to exercise equipment, and this is not what I made time in my schedule to hear.*

Now, imagine instead that your doctor gently suggests that exercising every day is a common challenge and one you are capable of overcoming with a little bit of help. And, let's say, on top of that, she hands you a list of resources including nearby gyms, affordable at-home exercise equipment you can buy such as a yoga mat, and maybe even lists a few home workout YouTube channels you can look into. It's likely that you'd feel better equipped and encouraged to make some healthy lifestyle changes than if your doctor had used the negative, "guilt tripping" strategy described previously.

Equally important to how doctors frame their advice is how they ask questions. Before doctors can know *what* to advise a patient, they first need to know what's going on. While having data from blood tests and other exams provide doctors with a rough idea of how a patient is faring, they can only learn the full story behind physiological symptoms from patients themselves. So, making sure to ask questions in a way that encourages open discussion rather than defensive secrecy is paramount to a successful doctor-patient conversation that leads to effective treatments.

Perhaps you've had the experience of sitting in a large lecture hall, puzzled by what your professor just finished explaining when she asks, "So, does anyone have questions?" Similarly, you may be well acquainted with the fear and hesitation that often accompanies an internal debate over whether you really want to ask a question in front of your boss and colleagues during the Q&A portion of a presentation.

If you're like me in these situations, you probably have some clarifying questions you want to ask, but feel a bit sheepish about doing so. When no one else jumped at the opportunity to question a conclusion or ask for a key concept to be repeated, you may have slumped back into your seat and satisfied yourself with jotting down a quick note about asking a question later.

A similar situation occurs when doctors ask patients if they have questions in a way that suggests actually venturing to pose a question is unwelcome. For example, a doctor's tone, body language, and overall demeanor can collectively imply that any patient who takes them up on their customary offer of "Do you have any questions?" is being disrespectful in challenging their authority and expertise. Or these rhetorical cues might suggest to a patient that asking questions reflects poorly on their competence and ability to understand basic medical information.

What if instead of asking "*Do* you have any questions?" doctors ask "So, *what* questions do you have for me?" Here, we're only changing one key word in the question: from "*do* you have" to "*what* questions do you have..." While it may seem unnecessary to pay such detailed attention to swapping out one word for another, this change is small but powerful.

Asking *if* the patient has questions can be intimidating. It can cause them to panic about what questions they should have but can't think of or silence those who are afraid of asking "stupid questions" in front of a highly educated professional. In contrast, doctors who ask *what* questions patients have are signaling with their rhetoric that they *expect* the patient to have questions.

If my teachers employed this strategy in class I would feel more validated in asking whatever question I have in my mind, even if it seems silly or insignificant. Similarly, teaching doctors to pay close attention to the rhetoric they use and what it implies can help them create a more welcoming environment for patients. Imagine the difference this can make for a patient who feels embarrassed or self-conscious asking about a symptom that seems "weird" or "disgusting." Chances are, many of these concerns are perfectly legitimate, and sometimes these seemingly small or potentially embarrassing health concerns are symptoms of a larger problem that needs to be addressed. So when patients feel empowered to ask a preventative "Is this a bad thing?" it can be the difference between an early skin cancer diagnosis and waiting ten years down the line until it's too late.

Avoiding stigmatizing language leads to better health outcomes

Unfortunately, there are many situations when doctors' careless rhetoric, or decision to not question the longstanding rhetoric medical professionals have used for years, can cost a patient precious time—and even their life.

The opioid epidemic has been ravaging the US for years. Drug overdose deaths affect every community, from Beverly Hills celebrities to small Midwestern towns to upper class metropolitan suburbs. Drug overdose deaths were four times higher in 2018 than in 1999, and in 2018, 70 percent of drug overdose deaths involved an opioid.[39] There's often a lot of social stigma surrounding drugs and drug overdoses, as author Beth Macy explores in her book *Dopesick*.[40] With so much stigma coming from parents, spouses, friends, and coworkers, the last person someone struggling with opioid addiction needs to receive further judgement from is their doctor.

Yet, because of the longstanding rhetorical habit of labeling those struggling with drug relapses as "failing" in their effort to get clean, patients often experience stigma from the very people who are supposed to be aiding them in their recovery. While medical providers have begun encouraging the public to view addiction as a disease that can be treated with proper medical help, oftentimes everyday medical rhetoric doesn't reflect this shift in perspective, and can hinder effective patient counseling.[41]

Victor Wu has a Masters of Public Health (MPH) and a Medical Degree (MD) from Emory University. In the past, he's worked as an adjunct professor and White House Fellow. Currently, Wu is the Chief Medical Officer of TennCare, Tennessee's Medicaid Agency. When I spoke with him, Wu highlighted how using rhetoric that emphasizes recovery rather than addiction struggles can better patient outcomes. Speaking in his own capacity and not on behalf of the state's,

---

39 Anonymous, "Understanding the Epidemic," *Centers for Disease Control and Prevention*, March 19, 2020.

40 Beth Macy, *Dopesick: Dealers, Doctors, and the Company That Addicted America* (Boston: Little, Brown and Company, 2018).

41 Mia Williams, "Addiction: Is It a Disease or a Choice?," Addiction Center, December 7, 2017.

Wu suggests integrating stigmatized medical terminology into the regular timeline of recovery, instead of using it as a stand-alone.

For example, instead of calling out a "relapse" as something abnormal, it should be mentioned often in conversations about addiction recovery to signal that it's not something to be ashamed of. This diminishes the stigma around the word and helps patients and family members normalize the fact that relapses are just one step on the road to recovery. "For a long time, we talked about relapse as someone that has...messed up," Wu said. "Like they weren't strong enough, or they weren't...emotionally able to really make it through their treatment."

To avoid giving off that connotation, Wu is careful to explain to patients that while he wants to work with them to prevent relapses from occurring, it's also a perfectly normal part of any recovery process and nothing to be discouraged about.

Unfortunately, not all doctors are as thorough in vetting their medical rhetoric. When doctors don't pay attention to their language, they often imply that "X" challenge is the patient's to solve, not theirs. Wu calls this tendency to put the burden of a flawless medical recovery on the patient's shoulders "blaming the patient." To avoid this, he likes to investigate any possible encouraging motives for recovery before informing patients of what they can do to better improve their health outcomes.

This can be as simple as having a fifteen-minute conversation about what else is going on in the patient's life, learning about their family, and maybe their past. Wu argues that as busy as they are, doctors have a responsibility to do their homework on a patient before seeking to persuade them to change their behavior. As we'll see in subsequent chapters, conducting a thorough investigation of your audience to better understand their background and motives is imperative to crafting a persuasive argument. Coming at a problem from your perspective is often ineffective and inefficient because your audience doesn't always share your perspective.

This is important for doctors to keep in mind. Whenever they make a recommendation, even a simple one involving what medicine to take and how often, doctors are seeking to persuade their patients. Whether they recognize it or not, doctors are essentially asking patients to trust them, trust that what they're saying is truly to the patient's benefit, and to trust that following their instructions will be worth it. From a doctor's perspective, it can be mind-boggling why some patients refuse to follow their recommendations. This is where making an effort to understand your audience (i.e., your patient) beforehand is invaluable.

For example, instead of getting frustrated at a patient struggling to take their medicine every morning like they're supposed to, and shaming the patient over her/his inability to perform this simple task, doctors can ask whether their patient's health is preventing them from pursuing any hobbies or tasks they enjoy.

Imagine you're a doctor and none of your pleading is getting across to your patient Ed. You've told him that he needs to remember to take his blood pressure medicine, otherwise he could suffer serious health consequences and even die.

But you're perplexed because Ed doesn't seem to have much motivation to take a few pills every day.

Instead of continuing to plead without aim, imagine if you took an extra ten minutes and asked Ed about what's happening in his personal life. In doing so, you find out some very pertinent information, including that while Ed doesn't have much personal motivation to keep an eye on his health, he is excited for his son's wedding in six months. Equipped with Ed's perspective and potential motivators, you can now explain to Ed the connection between taking his medicine daily and being able to see his son get married. In other words, by having a conversation with your patient and doing your "homework," you'll know how to best frame your medical advice in a way that maximizes Ed's likelihood of accepting it. Instead of wasting time and effort lecturing on the merits of taking blood pressure medicine, and trying to guilt Ed into following your advice, you'll be armed with the right perspective to use.

When he was still a young resident, Wu experienced the impact conducting "background research" on patients can have. At the advice of a senior resident, he took an extra ten minutes to sit down with a patient who consistently came in with medical risks due to his excessive drinking. It seemed like every few days Wu or his colleagues would tell this patient that his alcoholic behavior was unsustainable and that he was risking his life by continuing on like this. Like many other doctors, Wu assumed that this patient simply didn't care about his health. However, when he sat down and learned that the patient had gone through a lot of challenging times in his personal life, among them a lifelong regret of not having a closer relationship with his daughter, Wu realized that the rhetoric he had been using up till this point was all wrong.

Wu had been assuming that he knew the patient's thoughts and situation (i.e., he is simply an alcoholic and needs to be told the risks he's taking) and had been trying to advise this patient from a medical perspective on why alcoholism is threatening his health. Now, armed with a true motivator gleaned from his conversation with his patient (i.e., to live long enough to reconnect with his daughter), Wu was able to help the patient overcome his alcoholism and live a happier, healthier life. "Ultimately, health is just a manifestation of the underlying," Wu said. "Underlying stresses of your social situation, your job situation, education level, your family dynamic, traumatic childhood events; all these things feed into your health and health is at the manifestation of that. So, if you don't begin to engage with the person at that level and use the right language to invite them in to really talk about what's challenging for them, you're going to miss often on the diagnosis."

Just like how Tom Lee learned how important it is to not assume he knows what someone is feeling or thinking when trying to craft an accurate and effective article, Wu learned the importance of not assuming he knows where a patient is coming from. While his story had a happy ending, it could've ended differently. By framing their medical advice from the same perspective each time this patient came in (i.e., from their perspective as doctors), Wu and his colleagues had been wasting precious time during which the patient could've died from his alcoholism.

While not all of us are doctors, subtle differences in our language can strongly affect those around us, how they feel, and what actions they decide to take (or not). It's important to be wary of whether we use stigmatizing, discouraging, or dismissive language in our conversations with others to prevent hurting those we're trying most to help.

Why students should learn to master rhetoric before they become doctors

Many find it tempting to view doctors as scientists who only need to rely on their sharpened "hard skills" to be successful. Unfortunately, that viewpoint often leads educators and individuals already constrained by a vigorous science-based course schedule to overlook the importance of helping pre-medical students develop their rhetorical skills. As we've seen, avoiding stigmatizing language, arrogant body language, and learning to frame medical advice in a way that is appealing to the patient's inner motivations can have a significant positive impact on patients' health outcomes and also decrease doctors' frustration at "disobedient" patients.

All students, including pre-health students and medical school students, should be rigorously trained in how to refine their rhetoric in order to better serve their future patients. In a 1984 journal titled *The Humanities in Medical Education*, Dr. Kenneth Warren pointed out that although medical school applicants who major in the Humanities are few and far between, they had "the second highest overall acceptance rate," lagging behind physical science majors but closely tailed by Social Science students.

Undergraduates who majored in the Humanities (English, Philosophy, Foreign Language, Art, and/or Music) had an overall medical school acceptance rate of 51.2 percent in 1980. While this may not sound that high, Humanities majors' acceptance rates were higher than Natural Science majors (Biology, Chemistry, Physics, Biochemistry, Microbiology, and/or Zoology) who had an overall acceptance rate of 47 percent. In case you're curious, Social Science majors (Psychology, History, Economics, and/or Political Science) came in third with an overall acceptance rate of 43.8 percent. While this study may be a bit outdated, it reveals how beneficial it can be for future medical professionals to have significant training in the Humanities as undergraduate students where rhetoric often falls on the educational spectrum.[42]

This study provides some useful insight into how physicians have been thinking about the importance of a humanities-centered education for decades, but a more recent article published by the American Medical Association in 2019 reveals that doctors still agree that a humanities-centered education is uniquely equipped to help future doctors better serve their patients.[43]

Emergency Medicine physician Dr. Richard Ratzan credits a Classical-Greek-based education plan proposed by Dr. Lewis Thomas for inspiring his suggestion for how medical education can be reformed. Thomas was an American physician, poet, etymologist, educator, policy advisor, and researcher.

42 Kenneth S. Warren, "The Humanities in Medical Education," *Annals of Internal Medicine* 101, no. 5 (November 1, 1984): 697-701.

43 Richard M. Ratzan, "How to Fix the Premedical Curriculum—Another Try." *JAMA* 322, no. 8 (August 27, 2019): 710–711.

He believed that requiring pre-medical students to read and analyze classical works by Euripides, Sophocles, and other great writers in the original Greek is the optimal way for students to learn key qualities physicians must possess: empathy and "a language for compassion."

While this Classical Greek education proposal may sound a bit extreme and too rigorous to be practical, Thomas was essentially arguing that all doctors be trained to employ empathy-based rhetoric. Ratzan suggests that an English literature-focused curriculum that teaches medical students these rhetorical skills and provides them with a greater ability to empathize with the human condition is worth considering. Envisioning what such a curriculum would look like, Ratzan wrote, "All students applying for admission to medical school major in the humanities with an optional minor in biology and science topics. No pre-med majors need apply; the science training will come after acceptance. Any grounding in the humanities would suffice. As Thomas hinted, patients could look forward to being cared for by physicians 'who have learned as much as anyone can learn, in our colleges and universities, about how human beings have always lived out their lives.'"

Dr. John D. Schriner, an associate Dean of Admissions and Student Affairs at Ohio University Heritage College of Osteopathic Medicine, emphasizes the benefits of a humanities education that teaches medical students to be comfortable with the unknown. Most of the time, doctors are detectives using the same symptoms to diagnose a variety of ailments. In addition, medical care comes with a host of ethical dilemmas that doctors have to deal with, including what end of life care should look like, who should receive the best drugs and treatments, and the much debated "right to die" dilemma. "In medicine, things aren't just black and white or finite," Schriner said. "Some things are open for interpretation. A tolerance for ambiguity is a very positive quality in a medical student or a physician. You are not always going to have the answer, and you have to deal with things that are going to cause you to think with both your left and right brain."[44]

Dr. Marty Makary is the Chief of Islet Transplant surgery and a Professor of Surgery at Johns Hopkins. He agrees that medical education needs a redo. In addition to an MD, Makary holds a MPH and has written extensively about the flaws in the US healthcare system. In his most recent book, *The Price We Pay: What Broke American Health Care—and How to Fix It*, Makary argues that forcing students to memorize unnecessary microscopic details they can always look up on the internet later is a mistake and misallocation of scarce time. Rather, medical schools should incorporate classes that broaden future doctors' understanding of healthcare systems and how to communicate effectively with patients. "Medical education needs lipo," Makary wrote. "Instead of teaching every medical student how to refract people's eyes to fit them for eyeglasses, how about teaching them teamwork and communication skills?...I learned subatomic particles for the MCAT, but never learned how to explain diabetes at a sixth-grade reading level."[45]

---

44 Brendan Murphy, "How Humanities Background Could Make You a Better Medical Student," *American Medical Association*, March 5, 2020.

45 Marty Makary, *The Price We Pay What Broke American Health Care - and How to Fix It* (New York: Bloomsbury Publishing, 2019), 231.

But all hope is not lost. By incorporating mandatory courses on rhetoric and communication, schools can help doctors begin mastering their rhetoric right from the start and avoid adopting detrimental rhetorical habits that will harm patient health outcomes. If medical students get used to employing empathetic rhetoric that destigmatizes health conditions, they're much more likely to continue doing so once they become "official" doctors. Subsequently, they will be more likely to train their own residents and students to do the same. By instituting change at the pre-health educational level, the medical community can more seamlessly incorporate lessons on effective medical rhetoric and turn the emphasis on careful rhetoric from an anomaly to the norm.

While the essence of rhetoric is being able to be persuasive in any situation, it's a lot harder to be persuasive when you face a lot of uncertainties, time pressure, and haven't had adequate training to convey what you know and what you don't to patients in a way they can understand. By overloading students' schedules with STEM-only courses and undercutting the importance of taking communication-related classes beyond their mandatory first-year English class, universities are doing more than just under-preparing their pre-health students for the realities they'll face as practicing physicians. They're cheating future patients out of the optimal care they deserve.

Case study: "There's no evidence"

Now that we've gone over a few examples of why educating doctors on how to intentionally use rhetoric is important, let's take a look at the way scientists, doctors, and other health professionals rhetorically misled the public in the early days of the COVID-19 pandemic. As with any unfamiliar rapidly evolving situation, everyone's understanding of the virus and the latest science on it was constantly changing. Recognizing that, I'm not suggesting that any professionals gave false information on purpose or with malicious intent. However, as we've learned throughout this book, the rhetoric one uses can have far-reaching effects on the listener, whether it's intended or not, so it's important to learn from others' rhetorical mistakes so we can avoid them in the future.

Throughout their early reports, doctors and scientists used the phrase "there's no evidence" a lot.[46] Something that most scientists probably didn't consider is the significant difference between saying "there's no evidence" versus admitting that "we don't know." By saying "there's no evidence," doctors are framing their answer in a way that suggests that rigorous scientific studies have been conducted and they were able to come to a *conclusion* that there is no evidence of "X" concern or phenomenon.

But a more accurate way to respond to a journalist's probing questions would be to say, "we simply don't know at this point." One reason why doctors may have hesitated to frame things in such a blunt way is that it often feels uncomfortable to admit that you don't know something. As experts in the field and representatives of their colleagues on TV, it's understandable why doctors may have been particularly

---

46 Ed Yong, "Immunology Is Where Intuition Goes to Die," *The Atlantic*, August 5, 2020.

averse to admitting that they aren't able to offer the concrete public guidance they wish they could. Attempts to avoid an inevitable period of public panic can also cause doctors to shy away from clearly and accurately presenting what the scientific community does and does not know.

Makary also mentions the dangers of using the phrase "no evidence to support..." in his book. "The term...actually means one of two things: it's been studied and evidence does not support it, or it has not been studied and could be true," Makary wrote. "The liberal use of 'no evidence to support' has conditioned us to distrust anything not supported by trial. I've taught my students and residents to do better, replacing the sloppy phrase 'there is no evidence' with either 'It is unknown because it has not been adequately studied' or 'it has been studied adequately and has not been shown to be effective.'"[47]

As usual, the devil is in the details, particularly when it comes to rhetoric. Makary explains how using a phrase that suggests past studies have *concluded* that "X" treatment works (or doesn't) when, in reality, not enough research has been conducted, is a mistake many doctors make.

When properly used, "no evidence" should mean that no randomized control trials have been conducted. However, scientists' obsession with randomized control trials' robust design can lead them to view these trials as the only valid "evidence" of a treatment or phenomenon. This is problematic

---

47   Marty Makary, *The Price We Pay What Broke American Health Care - and How to Fix It*, 114.

because it can cause these scientists to make claims implying that no studies have been conducted instead of more accurately stating that insufficient or non-randomized studies have been conducted.[48]

Many medical questions, ranging from whether predatory insurance pricing exists to whether vaping has long-term negative effects cannot be answered with a randomized control trial for ethical and/or practical reasons. A lack of rhetorical awareness can lead doctors to the wrong conclusions and unreasonable standards to the detriment of patients and the overall medical community.

How can patients become more aware?

While it's important for doctors to be educated on rhetorical tools, it's equally important for us, as patients, to be on the lookout for the way medical rhetoric is used to promote or harm our health. While rhetoric can be used to encourage positive patient outcomes, it can also be wielded for more sinister purposes.

The US is notorious for having a complicated, expensive, and inefficient healthcare system.[49] Corporations contribute to the complications of US healthcare by using rhetorical tools

---

48 Maria Kabisch, et al. "Randomized controlled trials: part 17 of a series on evaluation of scientific publications." *Dtsch Arztebl Int.* 108, no. 39 (Sep 2011):663-668.

49 Tim Harford, "US Healthcare Is Literally Killing People," *Financial Times*, July 12, 2019.; Olga Khazan, "The 3 Reasons the U.S. Health-Care System Is the Worst," *The Atlantic*, June 22, 2018).

to intentionally mislead hospitals, doctors, and patients. Unfortunately, most patients are not aware of and/or paying attention to how treatments, drugs, and medical services are rhetorically framed, which can cause them to choose treatments that are more expensive, dangerous, and sometimes less effective than alternatives.

Makary extensively explores the various rhetorical pitfalls and tricks used by insurance companies, medical device sellers, and pharmaceuticals that make providing high-quality, affordable care so difficult in the US. Luckily, we can borrow his insider lens into the medical field to see what type of medical rhetoric we should be on the lookout for as consumers.

When you hear healthcare professionals presenting you with "costs" instead of "prices," you should perk up a little and pay closer attention to what information they're providing you with. While "costs" presents medical services from the perspective of providers, Makary argues that services should be framed in terms of "prices" when speaking with patients.[50]

If I'm a patient and a doctor is droning on about their costs, I might zone out, assuming this is the mundane procedural part I don't have to pay attention to. After all, costs are the hospital's problem, right? If I take this perspective, not paying much attention to the providers' word choice, I might be unpleasantly shocked back to life when I see my medical bill, only then processing that in referring to "costs" the providers were also indirectly referring to what I'll have to pay.

---

50   Marty Makary, *The Price We Pay What Broke American Health Care - and How to Fix It*, 234.

If instead a doctor presents me with information on prices, I'll be more likely to pay attention. Using "price" reminds consumers that if you agree to receiving a good or service, you're agreeing to pay for it and should expect some consequences if you end up unable to fulfill that promise. In addition, consumers are usually more strategic shoppers when they're the ones footing the bill, which can encourage patients to think twice about accepting an unnecessary treatment they can't afford. By using "prices," healthcare professionals will be more accurately conveying to patients exactly what they're signing up for, saving them a lot of unexpected financial trouble down the road.

Makary also describes how the term "preventable adverse event" is another example of how doctors use convoluted rhetoric in a harmful way. "The problem with this phrase, is that it doesn't make doctors or hospitals really claim responsibility for their mistakes when a procedure goes poorly. While the word 'preventable' is included, it is a term that washes everyone clean of responsibility, while the plainer terms express the truth a patient experiences," Makary wrote.[51]

All this misleading, indecipherable rhetoric and inaccurate word choice facilitates miscommunication in healthcare. A lack of clear communication as to why patients should pay attention leads to passive disengagement, which leaves patients vulnerable to being taken advantage of. "We need to start fixing healthcare by switching to a more honest lexicon…using the more accurate terminology in plain English would help change the conversation about healthcare. People

---

51   Marty Makary, *The Price We Pay*, 234.

could better understand what's really happening. It can also more effectively engage people with these important issues," Makary wrote.[52]

In medicine, a careless word, inability to effectively explain medical concepts to patients, or lost opportunity to better frame their advice can be the difference between life and death. That's why the ability to communicate effectively and convincingly should be taught, strengthened, and refined starting in future healthcare professionals' undergraduate days. Rather than being pushed aside in favor of cramming in more hard-science knowledge, developing doctors' rhetorical skills should be considered of equal, if not greater importance. After all, it's something our life could depend upon.

---

52   Marty Makary, *The Price We Pay*, 234-235.

Chapter 6

Finding the Magic Word

———

Rhetoric + Advertising

Have you ever seen a product advertised as "new" and "revolutionary" when it already exists? Perhaps it was under another brand name, at a different price point, or simply a different color than the original product. You may have wondered why anyone would spend the time, effort, and resources to rebrand an item. What is the point? As we'll learn in this chapter, advertisers rely heavily on rhetoric to repackage mundane items as an attractive "must have" or to make them stand for something new.

Because tech companies like Google have long been keeping tabs on what websites we are visiting and what products we're buying, we often get ads that are suspiciously relevant to our interests.[53] Sometimes, I find myself watching a full,

---

53 Todd Haselton, "How to Find out What Google Knows about You and Limit the Data It Collects," *CNBC*, December 6, 2017.

fifteen-second ad on why a new face serum is a must-have product instead of hitting the skip button. The ad draws me in with close-ups of the luxurious formula, animated explanations of moisture attracting molecules like hyaluronic acid, and some quick statistics on how many users felt their skin was more hydrated thanks to this new magical product. Then, the ad offers another reason to buy the serum: it comes in a recycled glass bottle.

While that may not sound as appealing to you as it did to me, it's pretty amazing how much advertisers are able to include about their product in just a few seconds. In the example above, advertisers were able to present four reasons why their product is a unique, must-have item and also made use of ethos to give prospective buyers yet another reason to purchase this product over another (i.e., to help protect the environment). I'm sure you can recall some pretty memorable ads you've seen, and when you've acted on your intrigue and bought the featured product. Because advertising focuses on capturing consumers' attention and convincing them that they need "X" item, having a strong grasp on rhetoric is an essential tool for those in the industry.

Jude Cohen is a strategist at Ogilvy, the New York City-based advertising, marketing, and public relations agency. When I spoke with her, she emphasized that understanding and helping brands harness the power of rhetoric is a key part of her work. Cohen highlighted the three basic rhetorical categories we learned about earlier on, ethos, pathos, and logos, as her rhetorical toolbox essentials. It may be more obvious how pathos is incredibly important in advertising, as advertisers strive to elicit strong emotions about a product, service, or cause so that consumers take action. Whether it's salivating at the Big Mac on the screen, all of a sudden feeling like your mouth is quite dry and in the mood for a Heineken, or rising anger at the way polar bears are going extinct, ads often evoke a visceral reaction in viewers. Drawing out and playing with people's emotions, and sometimes psychology, is a huge part of advertising.

But, with increasingly savvy and sometimes skeptical consumers, appealing to emotions is only one part of the puzzle. Providing logical reasons for why consumers should buy an item is another hurdle advertisers have to overcome with the help of rhetoric. Here, we're using the term "logic" broadly to refer back to "logos." Most of us are not going to just believe anything people say, especially if it's in an advertisement where we know the goal is to present things in the most favorable light possible and get us to reach into our wallets.

Depending on our personalities and how we think, some of us may prefer a graph or statistics and others might prefer testimonials from everyday consumers, while some may insist a product be celebrity approved. Whatever it is, advertisers strive to show individuals why buying their product is a reasonable, worthwhile purchase. Because consumers have a variety of personalities and ways of reasoning, advertisers play to what they think will make the most sense to their consumers. While this may not always be done with numbers and scientific explanations, or even actually follow the rules of logic, advertisers have to break down, in a matter of seconds, why it makes sense to purchase something.

The last strategy in this classic rhetorical trio, ethos, is one that Cohen feels strongly about and cited as a common pitfall for failed marketing campaigns. It's particularly damaging and distasteful when companies proclaim to have a certain value, or ethos, in their advertising but haven't shown a consistent history of action in a certain area. "One of my favorite things about working for brands, specifically in the social media space, is getting to educate them on the fact that this is no longer a one-way road in that consumers now also have a voice...[and] a platform," Cohen said. "And so, if your brand is not fully aligned in their logic and their reason to be in a specific space, you can bet you're going to hear about it from consumers...on social media."

Citing the rise in companies' commitment to Pride and supporting the LGBTQ+ community, Cohen emphasized how many savvy consumers do their research before buying a rainbow emblazoned product to confirm the company lives by their professed values. These consumers aren't just satisfied with declarations of support and rainbow goods in July. They want to make sure that companies are living out their proclaimed values year around. If consumers find inconsistencies between a company's advertising claims and their hiring practices, leadership, and day-to-day activities, consumers are not going to buy into a campaign.

In some cases, a company's failed campaign may achieve the opposite result they're hoping for and actually turn consumers away from a product and foster mistrust. "[If a company says] here's our logo on this product and we like the queer community now, people are [thinking], great, but what is rainbow Listerine going to do for me," Cohen said.

"If you're not fully mashing up on the values and the logic, then they're not going to buy into the campaign. They're not going to buy into your credibility and they're not going to buy your product."

Millennials and Gen Z consumers are especially cognizant of how they spend their money. Many younger consumers are wary of what companies they're backing with their wallet. Today, it's no longer enough to rely on pathos and logos alone to persuade consumers that your product is the best. According to a study by Accenture, Millennials alone spend around 600 billion dollars in the US each year. In 2020, Millennials are expected to spend 1.4 trillion dollars. And, according to research conducted by New York-based public relations company 5W, 83 percent of Millennials think it's important that the companies they purchase from have values that align with theirs.[54]

In fact, perhaps contrary to logos, Millennials are even willing to pay more for a product that has a stronger ethos argument than a cheaper product comparable in function and quality. For example, studies show that 73 percent of Millennials are willing to pay more for a product that is more sustainable.[55] With younger shoppers' increasing purchasing power and keen eye on a company's values, many companies have been striving to add more ethos to their campaigns.[56]

---

54 Anonymous, "Consumer Culture [5W PR 2020 Report] - NY PR Agency 5W Public Relations Blog," *5W Public Relations*, February 20, 2020.

55 Melanie Curtin, "73 Percent of Millennials Are Willing to Spend More Money on This 1 Type of Product," *Inc.com,* March 30, 2018.

56 Kai Johnson, "How Values-Driven Social Campaigns Help Businesses Make an Impact - Salesforce Blog," *Salesforce,* May 5, 2020.

Some brands, such as the cosmetics giant Sephora, are emphasizing racial and gender inclusivity. They launched their "We Belong to Something Beautiful" campaign that celebrated how diverse individuals share a love of beauty and makeup.[57] Other newer businesses, like women's intimates brand ThirdLove, have emphasized body inclusivity and independence.[58] ThirdLove has embraced comfortability and diverse body sizes in contrast to more traditional lingerie brands like Victoria's Secret that tend to have ads that emphasize a narrow range of "attractive" body types.[59] Men's grooming brand Axe also sought to encourage more diverse perspectives of masculinity with their "Find Your Magic" campaign.[60]

With values-based topics such as identity, racial, and size inclusivity becoming social movements and topics of widespread advocacy, companies need to adjust their rhetorical emphasis and ensure consistency across platforms. They need to not only profess their values, but convince consumers that they're in earnest. Successfully doing so depends on how skilled brands and advertising firms are on wielding rhetoric effectively.

57 Anonymous, "We Belong to Something Beautiful," Sephora.

58 Mary Hanbury, "Meet the Startup Founder Challenging the Way Women Shop for Bras," *Business Insider*, April 18, 2019.

59 Victoria Taylor, "Victoria's Secret's 'Perfect Body' Ads Draw Criticism," *NY Daily News*, October 29, 2014.

60 Curtis M. Wong, "Axe's New 'Find Your Magic' Ad Promotes A Different Type Of Masculinity," *HuffPost*, January 14, 2016.

Case Study: Understanding your audience matters

Jeff Goodby and Rich Silverstein are Co-Chairmen and Partners at San Francisco-based advertising firm Goodby, Silverstein, & Partners. Known for their critically acclaimed work, including the well-known "Got Milk?" and Budweiser Frogs campaigns, pro bono advertisements for causes including gun control, drinking and driving awareness, and national park conservation, among others, Goodby and Silverstein are giants in the advertising field.

How did they become so successful? Besides being a complimentary writer/designer duo, they encourage a respect and understanding of language in their firm. They recognize that without skilled rhetoric, they cannot succeed as advertisers. "Our job is to distill what [clients] know into a magic word, or words," Silverstein said.[61]

Silverstein and Goodby like to describe ads as short, sixty-second films. As concise as they are, ads still have to hit all the right emotional notes, follow a storyline, and leave the reader with a memorable impression. Condensing important information into such a short time frame means advertisers have to be efficient. When every second counts, knowing which words are necessary, and what you can cut, is important. Being able to skillfully differentiate between language that contributes significantly to getting your message across, and what can be conveyed with an

---

61   Jeff Goodby and Rich Silverstein, "Working With Brands," in "Jeff Goodby & Rich Silverstein Teach Advertising and Creativity," MasterClass, November 13, 2020, video, 6:28.

image or body language instead, requires having a solid mastery of rhetoric.

Having studied English at Harvard as an undergraduate student, Goodby is no stranger to writing and rhetoric. Goodby enjoys the creative liberty writers have in the advertising field to "break the rules," but emphasizes that before writers break the rules, they need to know why they're doing it. He suggests adopting unconventional language only if advertisers are keenly aware of how it's helping get the ad's point across better.

Learning to wield language creatively yet effectively requires a sophisticated rhetorical toolbox. Goodby encourages writers to constantly broaden their linguistic skills and ability to convey what they intend by immersing themselves in language, different people's perspectives, and avoiding becoming enamored with one specific writing style. "If you're going to take liberty with the language, you have to have a reason to do it," Goodby said. "Read a lot of stuff because that's the raw material of what you're doing and it teaches you about the people you'll be speaking to, that you have to write to."[62]

In order to run a successful firm, Goodby and Silverstein also need to constantly sell their ideas, talent, and services to potential clients. As we'll discuss further in our chapter on law, our body language, tone, and nonverbal cues are aspects of our rhetoric that are just as important, and sometimes even more important, as the content we're conveying.

---

62 Jeff Goodby and Rich Silverstein,"On Craft: Writing, Design, and Giving Direction," 0:48.

In their early days, Goodby and Silverstein underestimated the importance of understanding their audience and adjusting themselves accordingly. Once, they almost lost a German client because they took off their suit jackets and didn't stand up when they spoke, which their client considered rude and unprofessional. Being two casual Californians, they made an honest mistake. But, after that experience, and some pointers from friends about how their presentation needs to be adjusted to their audience (in this case, to accommodate differing cultural norms), Goodby and Silverstein are wary of how their nonverbal cues are complementing or distracting from the high-quality content they're trying to sell to a client.

Knowing yourself and how you tend to speak, hold yourself, or dress is also an important part of refining the supporting nonverbal aspects of your rhetoric. "How you perform, how you present it, is just as important as what the script says or what the idea is," Silverstein said. "How you dress, how you come across, is it their room or your room, it matters."[63]

Knowing how to frame content for a wide variety of clients also serves them well as bosses. Many employees dread receiving critical feedback. For those in creative industries, receiving feedback can be especially hurtful because the work they're presenting is often deeply personal and in some ways an expression of themselves. When singers are rejected from an audition, they can feel like the judge is dismissing their voice—literally. Or, when a painter's work is dismissed as "nothing special," they might see the months they spent

---

63   Jeff Goodby and Rich Silverstein,"It's Great, but They'll Never Buy It: Selling a Crazy Idea," 5:20.

working on it flash before their eyes. This may sound a bit dramatic to some, but this just goes to reinforce the importance of framing feedback according to the listener's personality in order for it to be as helpful as possible. "You go ok, this person needs a lot of explanation, this person doesn't need a lot of explanation," Goodby said. "This person is very visual, this person likes to hear stories…there are different people on the other side of the table for all of these jobs and you have to take that into account."[64]

Like Cohen, Goodby and Silverstein are also passionate about helping brands effectively express their moral values to their audience. "I think more than anything it says a brand has a soul, has some toughness, and stands by beliefs," Silverstein said.[65]

But showing audience members a brand's "soul" is not an easy task. Ads have to come across as genuine, sincere, and touch viewers emotionally. While it's heartwarming to see viewers' positive responses to value-themed advertisements, such as the Rainbow Pride Dorito Chip ad they produced, Silverstein also emphasizes the importance of making sure the brand lives up to their claims. Advertisers are responsible for making sure their clients succeed and that often means making sure they don't overcommit or state something that will prove all talk and no action. "You can't just holler and say we're for something, you have to do something, there has to be a cause and effect," Silverstein said.[66]

---

64 Jeff Goodby and Rich Silverstein,"It's Great, but They'll Never Buy It," 7:54.
65 Jeff Goodby and Rich Silverstein,"Advertising Is Everything… and Everything Is Advertising," 3:31.
66 Jeff Goodby and Rich Silverstein,"Advertising Is Everything," 4:07.

Advertising isn't just about knowing how to use language to persuade others. In addition to the need to understand the basics of rhetoric like ethos, logos, and pathos, knowing how (and why) to go against mainstream language is also important in crafting a memorable ad. As an advertiser, gaining a deep understanding of yourself, team members, clients, and audience is also essential to guiding how you frame and present critical information. Once advertisers have a solid grasp on written rhetoric, their work has only just begun.

Rhetorically based from the start

While advertising may seem like an endless game of toying with our emotions, reasoning, and values, it's a field whose foundations are built on becoming more persuasive than the competition by letting audiences guide their rhetorical choices. For some audiences, a logical appeal will be the most effective, while for another ethos is needed to hit the mark. While different ads have varying balances of these three elements, how did pathos come to dominate almost every ad?

The advertising industry is huge with more than \$560 billion spent worldwide in 2019.[67] While the idea of "American consumerism" began after World War II in the 1940s, today we still live in a society that values buying new goods, often those we don't need, over durable ones that we can use for years.[68] Before the 1940s, most American consumers only bought goods that were considered "necessities" and such practical

---

67 A. Guttmann, "Advertising Market Worldwide - Statistics & Facts," *Statista*, January 15, 2021.

68 Anonymous, "The Rise of American Consumerism," *PBS*.

spending was the norm at the time. While the wealthy classes were used to buying luxury items, it wasn't until the 1940s that mass consumerism came into play. Advertisers shifted from framing items as functional, logical buys to heightening their emotional appeal.

These pathos-based ads are something we're all pretty used to and one of the fundamental advertising building blocks we learned from Cohen. But, to understand how and why advertising became so rhetorically pathos-heavy, we have to step back in time to meet the founder of modern-day advertising strategies: Edward Bernays.

While the name Bernays may not ring a bell, Freud likely does. Sigmund Freud was an Austrian neurologist and founder of psychoanalysis. Freud's psychoanalytic theory was revolutionary and focused on humans' unconscious desires. Intrigued by his uncle's theories on how these desires affect people's behavior in ways they often don't realize, Bernays capitalized on the idea that people have various unconscious needs and desires to create a new way of advertising.[69]

Seeking to invent a new way to sell products to consumers that focused on how a product could make a consumer feel, Bernays turned to his experiences using pathos-based rhetoric for war propaganda. When he was only twenty-six years old, Bernays was invited to the Paris Peace Accords that ended World War I alongside President Woodrow Wilson.[70]

---

69 *Encyclopædia Britannica Online*, Academic ed., s.v. "Psychoanalytic Theory," accessed February 23, 2921.

70 History.com Editors, "Paris Peace Accords Signed," *History.com*, last updated May 12, 2020.

He attained this high honor with his rhetorical prowess as he coined the infamous phrase "make the world safe for democracy," successfully using political rhetoric to portray Wilson as a world-saving hero.[71] After seeing firsthand how successful his tagline was as evidenced by Wilson's warm welcome in Paris, Bernays turned his attention to how he could use similar rhetorical techniques for business purposes.

First, Bernays recognized that the connotations of "propaganda" were becoming increasingly negative, particularly after fascist and communist governments started using it.[72] So, to avoid saying he creates "propaganda" for a living, Bernays cleverly coined a new phrase: public relations. Bernays' intentional coinage of a new term to elevate his work, even though the work itself didn't change, reveals how Bernays was extremely aware of the impact rhetoric can have. Under the title of a "public relations" company, Bernays built a fortune off advertising by framing certain products as the material manifestations of current social movements and ideals.

His first advertising campaign was a hit, although not for the most honorable cause. While smoking was popular in the 1940s, it was still taboo for women to smoke. Bernays wondered if he could use advertising to convince women to do the irrational: to take up smoking despite widespread societal disapproval. Unfortunately for women's health, Bernays achieved his goal.

---

71 Anonymous, "Woodrow Wilson," *The White House*, accessed January 15, 2021.

72 "The Story of Propaganda: AHA," *American Historical Association*, accessed January 15, 2021.

By staging a one-time symbolic ad, showing young women openly smoking, alongside the phrase "torches of freedom," Bernays successfully linked smoking to the women's suffrage movement. After his campaign, the number of women who smoked increased dramatically, and smoking itself became associated with being powerful and independent. With the successful effects of his rhetorical campaign that appealed to a "logical" reason to smoke (i.e., stand up for your rights) and an emotional aspect (i.e., you'll feel more like an independent woman), Bernays was off to the races.

Bernays was taken aback at his successful ad campaign because it was based on a simple appeal to human desires. He was surprised at how easily he was able to evoke to women's desires to be equal members of society by relying heavily on emotional appeal rather than logic and reason (which were how most ads were framed at the time). It dawned on Bernays, and soon American corporations, that another equally, if not more effective way to sell products is to proffer it to consumers' emotions and desires, not their brain.

Ultimately, Bernays showed corporations how they could make people want things they didn't need by linking items to their inner desires making them "happy and therefore docile."[73] This discovery sparked a shift from advertising the practicality of items to encouraging consumers to subconsciously form emotional links between products and their desire to express themselves in a certain way to others. You can thank Bernays for your desire to own a Rolls-Royce when

---

73 *Adam Curtis Documentary*, "The Century of Self," YouTube video (Documentary).

you finally "make it" or an Italian villa you renovate for millions of dollars and show off to your college friends. Bernays became so well-off that he ended up supporting Freud, who suffered financial hardship due to Vienna's economic downturn later in his life.

While these advertising strategies may sound a bit concerning and are in some ways a "monster" that even Bernays admitted to creating, I want to emphasize this key takeaway: rhetoric is at the core of advertising, and whether we like it or not, we're constantly bombarded with powerful rhetorical tools in ads. So, if you want to be a savvier and more informed consumer, now you know how advertisers get it done.[74]

---

74 Tim Adams, "How Freud Got under Our Skin," *The Guardian*, March 10, 2002.

Chapter 7

Putting Yourself on the Map

Rhetoric + Business

Have you ever wondered why there are seemingly infinite variations of titles for the same job? How is an "assistant director" different from an "associate director" or an "analyst" different from an "associate?" Such office rhetoric is widely used to give differing connotations as to the prestige of one role relative to another or to differentiate how one employee's responsibilities differ slightly from another. Whatever the reason, rhetoric is used by companies in the business world to separate themselves from their competitors. Because specific terms hint to outsiders how they should view a company, service, or product, they are intentionally shaped to match what a company wants to convey about itself; how they want consumers to respond.

When you think about the word "business," huge tech companies that have defined our modern day lives and workplaces, such as Google and Facebook, are probably some of the first companies that come to mind. The tech industry has earned renown not only for their innovative, life-changing technologies, but also for their progressive workplaces that allow everything from nap pods, to five months of paid maternity leave, to free snacks and catered lunches.[75] But, the tech industry's close attention to office rhetoric is perhaps one of the more overlooked yet highly impactful aspects of its culture.

At Google, there is no "Human Resources" (HR) department. Rather, you'll find a robust "People Operations" team. While you might be tempted to write off the switch from "human" to "people" as Google's effort to merely distinguish themselves as a newer, "hip" company, given what we've learned about rhetoric there's more to it than that.

When you think about the term "human resources," your mind might conjure up imagery of a group of monotonous workers mercilessly managing the company's hundreds of employees including giving out routine dismissal notices. On the other hand, the phrase "people operations" imparts a sense of laissez faire management with an emphasis on workers' individuality.

Google doesn't just stop with a department name change. They carry over their respect for the contributions each

75 Anne Cassidy , "Clocking off: the Companies Introducing Nap Time to the Workplace," *The Guardian*, December 4, 2017; Kristen Lotze, "10 Tech Companies with Generous Parental Leave Benefits," *TechRepublic*, February 15, 2019; Áine Cain, Hollis Johnson, and Sarah Jacobs, "Free, Unlimited Snacks Are Becoming a Common Office Perk - Here's How Companies like Facebook and LinkedIn Feed Their Employees," *Business Insider*, December 8, 2016.

individual brings by referring to workers not as "employees" but as "our people." Collectively, the new and improved office rhetoric Google employs helps present a favorable image of a company that recognizes the value in each and every one of their workers and thinks of them as not just employees but a part of the Google "family."

The use of "family" is a helpful rhetorical tool that many other companies use as well. Phrases such as "join the family" assures prospective employees that they'll be valued not only for their skill sets but as a person. Similar to how "people'" helps humanize workers and foster a sense of individuality at Google, using "family" is a way companies create office rhetoric that conveys an endearing, almost parental, sense of care about employees' personal lives and professional development.

It's also likely that Google's unique terminology for its HR department is an effort to differentiate their data-based hiring strategies from the more qualitative methods "traditional" companies use. Unlike many companies that rely on "soft" interpersonal cues, such as reputation and trust, to make people-management decisions, Google relies on "people analytics." Although it's not surprising that a company built on data integrates data into its everyday operations, Google's approach to incorporating data into people-management decisions is considered revolutionary.[76]

While most companies are hesitant to quantify people's feelings and preferences, Google capitalized on its superior data

---

76   John Sullivan, "How Google Reinvented HR and Drives Success through People Analytics," *Inside HR*, November 27, 2013.

capabilities to ensure there's always a quantitative basis for their decisions. No aspect of the company is too small for data, as they rely on it to decide everything from how much "free time" employees should get, to whether offering free food to employees is worth the cost, to how to best increase retention and diversity within the company. Instead of having to rely on the ambiguity of whether employees "agree" or "strongly agree" with a proposal, an analytics-based approach allows Google's people ops to turn wishy-washy opinions into concrete algorithms that can be applied to any situation.

With such a different approach to people management, it is perhaps clearer why Google is insistent on using a completely different set of terms for HR-related activities. Giving something a distinct name sends a rhetorical signal to the public that they're doing something different. This is particularly impactful when a practice has existed in some form in the past. In the case of "people operations," Google created a term that not only highlighted the value of their employees as unique contributing individuals, but also successfully distinguished itself from the more archaic and arguably ineffective types of HR management associated with older, more traditional companies.

Creating tools to help individuals improve their office rhetoric

In 2020, Microsoft released a set of new Artificial Intelligence (AI) tools that help users improve the quality and accuracy of their writing. For anyone who has ever spent hours typing out essays on Word, you might be feeling a little jealous that this tool just came out recently. But, what's particularly interesting about this host of new AI tools is that they were created with extreme rhetorical intentionality and detail in order to support the diverse ways people use language, as well as the diverse types of people using Microsoft's programs.

Microsoft Office now offers spell check in eighty-nine languages, has become 15 percent more effective in catching common errors made by those with dyslexia, and has even created an inclusive language critique. Recognizing the power of rhetoric and the impact using (or avoiding) specific words can have, Microsoft routinely works with native speakers and linguistic experts in twenty languages to guide their editing suggestions and also get a sense for what inclusive critiques don't fit certain languages or cultures.[77]

For their most recent update, Microsoft worked with a wide variety of professionals, ranging from philosophers to engineers, in an effort to be intentional about what data sets they use to train their AI, run through possibilities in which people could be indirectly affected by their technology, and to identify any ways people could be unintentionally harmed by designs that don't consider a broader range of needs. While this may all seem like a lot of work for a word processing program, Microsoft's emphasis on developing an inclusive AI editing program reveals their recognition of how important rhetoric is in users' everyday lives. It also reveals their desire to provide users with a tool to help them become more cognizant of what their everyday rhetoric implies.

---

77 Jennifer Langston, "New AI Tools Help Writers Be More Clear, Concise and Inclusive in Office and across the Web," *Microsoft: The AI Blog*, March 30, 2020.

Let's run through a quick scenario that will clarify how the new inclusive critique function can help users better express what they intend to say by suggesting more effective rhetoric. Imagine you're applying to be a Venture Capitalist at Sequoia. The world of finance, like many business industries, still tends to be majority male, especially at the top. So it would be a reasonable assumption to assume your future boss is male.[78] But, even if you didn't make that strategic calculation and made a more on-the-whim decision to employ the societally conditioned default "he" or "him" in your cover letter, let's see how Microsoft AI's inclusiveness critique function could help you be more careful of your rhetoric, leading to higher chances of a successful application.

When you're writing your cover letter after a long day at work, you might be jittery, exhausted, and/or mentally drained. You're also probably more focused on what you want to say instead of how you're conveying your ideas. That state of mind could lead you to emphasize how you are able to "man-up" when it comes to tackling challenges without a second thought. Due to societal conditioning and implicit bias, your brain could easily overlook such gendered language and encourage you to keep typing away.[79]

After a sleepless night, you finally send off your application and wait anxiously for the results. But, little did you know

78 Stacey Chin, Alexis Krivkovich, and Marie-Claude Nadeau, "Closing the Gap: Leadership Perspectives on Promoting Women in Financial Services," *McKinsey & Company*, September 6, 2018.

79 Carlos David Navarrete, et al., "Fear Extinction to an Out-Group Face: The Role of Target Gender," *Psychological Science* 20, no. 2 (February 2009): 155–58.; Dr. Pragya Agarwal, "Here Is How Unconscious Bias Holds Women Back," *Forbes*, December 17, 2018.

that the hiring manager who skimmed through your cover letter is female and was put off by the way "man up," (i.e., your rhetoric) suggests that rising up to the occasion is associated with men rather than women. That's strike one. But, let's assume the hiring manager is feeling generous that day and cuts you some slack. She sends your cover letter, resume, and application to your potential future boss.

Now, this potential future boss—let's call her Lucy—has dedicated her career to increasing the number of women in upper-level finance. This includes everything from intentionally seeking more female candidates, to hosting "women in finance" conferences and mentoring younger women at the company. Lucy opens your resume and is impressed. She then proceeds to read your cover letter, which is when her smile fades into a frown. Lucy's thinking, *I've spent my whole life trying to educate my colleagues about gender bias in the workplace and trying to diversify our firm. How can I possibly benefit from hiring someone who is going to perpetuate the damaging gender stereotypes that already consume the finance industry? That goes against everything I stand for!*

You may be protesting that in this scenario the applicant didn't mean to offend anyone and just hadn't thought about the impact using a gendered term could have. And I agree with you; an honest mistake is probably what happened. But, we are all held accountable to the language we use whether it's our most well-written, edited speech, or a rushed memo written while draining your fifth cup of coffee that day. Tech companies like Microsoft that are actively creating tools to encourage us to be more wary of our rhetoric in our everyday communications may seem "unnecessarily progressive," but they stand to benefit us all.[80]

Case Study: How to use rhetoric like a boss

Now that we know how businesses use rhetoric to shape their image and help consumers better shape theirs, let's take a look at how business leaders use rhetoric to effectively accomplish their goals. Industry leaders are often responsible for not only guiding their own company, but a whole conglomerate of assets and competitors in the field. With thousands, and sometimes millions, of individuals looking to them for guidance, it's imperative that business leaders are well-versed in rhetoric.

CEOs in particular need to know how to win people over. They often have to convince reluctant board members to support bold ventures and have faith in them even during setbacks. CEOs also need to constantly negotiate with employees, stockholders, and colleagues.

To see how rhetoric comes into play for these key business leaders, let's take a look at how former Disney CEO Bob Iger used rhetoric to inspire his team members who run ESPN, Disney Parks, Disney Animation, Pixar Animation, Marvel, and Lucasfilm, among other influential media assets. As the head of the Disney conglomerate for fifteen years, Iger has a sophisticated rhetorical toolkit he's refined over the years.[81]

---

80 Harris, Chelsea A et al. "What is in a Pronoun? Why Gender-fair Language Matters," *Annals of surgery* 266, no.6 (2017): 932-933.

81 "Robert A. Iger," The Walt Disney Company, accessed February 3, 2021.

As a leader, Iger has tried many different ventures, some of which, like acquiring Pixar Animation, have led to greater success, while others, including a TV cop musical, have failed. In light of his experiences and how his former bosses treated his "honest mistakes," Iger emphasized the importance of expressing humility and owning up to your mishaps when they happen. "There's great value in being candid and acting accountable, and taking responsibility," Iger said.[82]

Instead of hiding behind defensive, executive-level rhetoric that admits to some wrongdoing yet denies it at the same time, Iger suggests using straightforward rhetoric. Letting everyone know that "X" mistake happened demonstrates transparency and humility and allows everyone to move forward. This is a strategy Dr. Makary also suggested when he encouraged doctors to avoid using dismissive language such as "preventable adverse event" that absolves them of responsibility. Owning up to mistakes reassures team members of leaders' dedication, honesty, and humility. And, as we'll see in our chapter on politics, retaining and building trust is one of the most important assets a leader can have.

Using direct rhetoric that builds trust is also an essential in negotiation and making deals. Most leaders who reach the C suite (i.e., CEO, COO, CFO) have been in the industry for years, and over time, others learn about leaders' reputations. This can include whether they're known as a straight-shooter or tricky maneuverer. In Iger's experience, it's much easier

82   Bob Iger, "Tenets for Success" in Bob Iger Teaches Business Strategy and Leadership, November 13, 2020, MasterClass video, 7:59.

working with fellow business leaders when he's straightforward about what he can bring to the table.

Over his career, Iger made four main acquisitions that strengthened Disney, adding substantially to the brand: Pixar Animation, Marvel Studios, Lucasfilm, and 21st Century Fox. For many of these acquisitions, people thought there was no way Iger could close a deal, either because the founders or current CEOs of the companies could never bear to part with their creations and/or because of the high selling price expected. But Iger pulled off all four. How? By using direct, clear rhetoric from the start. This helped him build a trusting relationship with potential business partners and helped move negotiations along in a timely manner. There was no guessing where his mind was at or what he was able to offer.

Steve Jobs in particular appreciated Iger's direct communication. "There was a spirit of candor at the negotiating table that he truly appreciated," Iger said. "He realized there wasn't a game being played. Instead, there was a discussion and negotiation with an absolute result in mind."[83]

Note how Iger came into the negotiation with a clear end goal in mind. This emphasis on knowing what you want before you even begin speaking is something we'll explore more in-depth in our chapter on law. With a concrete business aim as his North Star, Iger was able to be upfront with potential business partners because he knew where his indisputable limits and goals were.

---

83   Bob Iger, "The Art of Negotiation," 3:39.

Now, imagine you're negotiating a merger between your bookstore café business and your friend Sarah's gourmet popcorn business. What if Sarah told you something like: "Well, maybe I could give you three of my stocks for each of your stock. But I'll get back to you on that. I can't make any promises, but I guess it could happen."

Do you see how wishy washy that language is? Sarah is asserting that something could be a possibility, but is not clear about how likely she'll actually trade at a 3:1 ratio. The use of "could" and "I guess" reveal that either she is genuinely not sure what she can offer you or (more likely) that she's not going to be upfront with you about where her head is at. This makes it really hard for you to gauge how keen Sarah is to sell and perhaps makes you wonder whether she's serious about a potential deal at all. Contrast that statement with this one:

"You know I really value your bookstore café. It's a community staple, and our partnership has the potential to add something unique to both of our ventures. I'm willing to give you two of my stocks for one of yours. I know that's a bit lower than you're looking for, but that's the best I can do. But I can promise you that I will respect the current culture and structure of the cafés. So, what do you think?"

This second response is much clearer and straight to the point. Most importantly, it anticipates and answers three main points of concern: First, does Sarah value your business? Second, how much is she willing to pay for it (in this case, in equity)? Third, will she attempt to overthrow your hard work once she acquires your cafés or will she be respectful of your current team?

This type of direct rhetoric that leaves very little ambiguity is the type of communication Iger recommends leaders use. Not only does it speed the negotiation process along, but it also saves you and your business partners a lot of "what ifs." And, as the saying goes, time is money. Being clear and upfront rhetorically is also a sign of respect. By putting their cards on the table with clear language, leaders demonstrate confidence in themselves, respect for their potential business partner, and express a genuine desire to make a deal.

Being clear about his expectations for company employees is also a top priority of Iger's and one of his keys to success. As we've seen, learning to communicate clearly and concisely is harder than it sounds, but it's an essential to mastering rhetoric and effective leadership. "A strategy is only as good as your ability to communicate it," Iger said. "Clarity becomes incredibly important. Clarity is actually an essential ingredient to good leadership as well. When you lead people, you need to be very, very, clear about what you expect of them."[84]

Iger also emphasized how it's important to understand your bosses' personality as well as team members'. This idea of knowing your audience will resurface throughout this book, and for good reason. In order to know how to frame your opinion in a persuasive way, you need to know where the other person is coming from. In his book, *The Ride of a Lifetime,* Iger cited several experiences where he appealed to his superiors' pride in their work and the company to encourage them to try something new.

---

84   Bob Iger, "Focus, Strategy, and Priorities," 4:10.

Imagine you're at a Fortune 500 company and your boss's name is Emily. Emily is a perfectionist. She's hard on herself and her team members, but not because she's uncaring. It's clear to all her employees that she's obsessed with making sure customers receive the best products, and that impacts her attitude towards others. She's also a reasonable person, but favors logical arguments over emotional ones (i.e., logos over pathos). Armed with this brief overview of Emily's work personality, imagine you are trying to get her to endorse new endeavor that is a bit out of the box: getting a company fleet of Teslas so you all can use them for "business purposes." How should you approach this?

Your best shot is framing your request in the most logical way possible, explaining how it's really a need, not a want, and tying in how it will help you (and your colleagues) achieve Emily's end goal: 100 percent customer satisfaction in product quality. You could begin by paying Emily some sort of compliment or congratulating her on a recent successful company launch. This will prime her to be more receptive to whatever you say next. Because Emily prides herself on achieving superior business results, making a comment showing you recognize her efforts will score you some brownie points.

Then, you could get down to business and explain why this Tesla fleet is in her best interest. The conversation could go something like this:

"Hi, Emily. I just wanted to pop in and say congrats on the successful tablet launch! I know it was your top priority these past few years, and it's really cool to see how it came to fruition. While I'm here, I had a quick idea I wanted to run by you." Hopefully, at this point, Emily is looking like she's in a pretty good mood and isn't glancing at the clock, her phone, or both. If she does seem a bit annoyed, it's probably a good time to throw in some encouraging nonverbal cues, such as flashing a dashing smile.

Next, you could move forward with something like this: "So, I was thinking how we can best achieve customer satisfaction. We know that we put our all into creating the best products and customer experiences possible, but how are our customers going to know that if they don't have the chance to meet with us and see our passion for our products? I'm thinking that if we had a company Tesla fleet, employees could take turns visiting our high-end customers in person. This will help us build strong personal ties, foster customer loyalty, and also give us a chance to address any concerns. I know our top competitor uses a similar strategy and customers appreciate the personal touch a lot."

It might sound a bit overboard, but with some skilled delivery and logically sound connections, you'll be on your way to convincing Emily to listen to another five minutes of your pitch and maybe agree with you on the spot.

Let's wrap up our exploration of business leader rhetoric with another nuanced tip from Iger. When encountering resistance to change, Iger suggests using specific word choice to differentiate strategic change from careless change. Working at a company whose major selling point is the nostalgia of childhood, Iger explains why he is careful to distinguish between "reverence" and "respect" when speaking with colleagues. Particularly at a company with an emotionally charged legacy, Iger discussed how it can be tricky to get people on board with decisions that can be seen as tarnishing the brand, even if these decisions will help the company remain competitive. As a Disney fan, I can attest to the fine line between an "innovation or die" pitch and the seemingly disingenuous advocacy to encompass more genres and fans simply because it's a smart business move.

That's why Iger pays detailed attention to explaining the difference between *revering* the past and *respecting* it. "Disney's brand needed to be respected, but not revered," Iger said. "And there's a big difference. If you revere something, then you work hard to protect it so that it stays the same. And if you do that you might as well just put it in a museum case so that it doesn't change and so no one can touch it."[85]

As you can imagine, it's difficult to shore up a brand to face the challenges of the technological age if people are convinced that reverence is the only option. Reverence prevents change, and as the old saying goes, change is the only constant in the world. Tasked with making Disney relevant to a new generation, and in a new technological age, Iger relied on rhetoric to assuage team members' fears about his many acquisitions and technological innovations; he convinced them that he was still "respecting" the past even though he was shoring up the company to face new challenges. "If you respect a brand versus revere it, then you're considering all the reasons why it was valuable in the first place," Iger said. "You're doing so in a way that brings those values, those qualities forward but enables it to change and be relevant

---

85 Bob Iger, "Creating Brand Value," 5:27.

in a world that is substantially different than the world that existed when the brand was created."[86]

By introducing and sticking to two separate terms when describing and explaining his choices, Iger helped clarify the difference in employees' minds, whose support was essential to his successful acquisitions.

Case Study: Rhetoric guides career advancement for female executives

We've seen how industry giants use rhetoric in their day-to-day activities, but those of us who haven't reached our career peak can also use rhetoric to speed our journey along. Hannah Riley Bowles is the Roy E. Larsen Senior Lecturer in Public Policy and Management at Harvard Kennedy School, where she chairs the Management, Leadership, and Decision Sciences (MLD) Area and co-directs the Women and Public Policy Program. Bowles has over twenty-five years of experience in negotiation and conflict management training, practice, and research. Her current research focuses on women's leadership advancement.[87]

In a paper titled "Claiming Authority: How Women Explain their Ascent to Top Business Leadership Positions," Bowles breaks down two main ways women justified their career ascent: A) By following the well-traveled road to career advancement (i.e., high performance leads to promotions)

---

86 Bob Iger, "Creating Brand Value," 5:51.
87 "Hannah Riley Bowles," Women and Public Policy Program, Harvard Kennedy School, accessed February 4, 2021.

or B) appealing to "gatekeepers of social hierarchy" through effective self-advocacy.[88]

For her paper, Bowles, examined the career paths of fifty female executives in both traditional major corporations and entrepreneurial ventures. When I spoke with her, Bowles emphasized the role persuasive narrative storytelling plays in helping women advance in a more unconventional manner (path B). Because these women refuse to follow the "normal" bureaucratic avenues of career progression, they need to be able to explain why they deserve a special path. "It starts with a kind of impact that they want to have or some difference that they want to make," Bowles said. "They lead with a story, and the way they develop their authority is by becoming one of the most persuasive storytellers around this issue. And it's not only pointing out the issue, but typically, hopefully, pointing to some form of solution. And so they usually will bring in some degree of their personal narrative."

In other words, rhetoric is what helped some of these female executives reach the C-suite more quickly than their counterparts who worked their way through the ranks in a traditional manner. Those who take path A are hoping that gender discrimination and the glass ceiling won't hold them back from attaining the positions they deserve.[89] However, this traditional route has its pitfalls, as gender stereotypes encourage discriminatory behavior in the workplace,

---

88 Hannah Riley Bowles, "Claiming Authority: How Women Explain their Ascent to Top Business Leadership Positions," *Research in Organizational Behavior* 32 (2012): 189–212.

89 David A. Cotter, Joan M. Hermsen, Seth Ovadia, Reeve Vanneman, "The Glass Ceiling Effect," *Social Forces* 80, no. 2 (December 2001): 655–681.

including how "women are ill equipped to succeed in traditionally male positions."[90]

So, the female executives who are able to use narrative storytelling to persuade "gatekeepers" of the current social hierarchy, which can include bosses and investors, that they belong at a higher place on the totem pole are much better positioned to advance successfully, and quickly, in their careers. Storytelling is a powerful and complex rhetorical tool that professionals can use to better persuade their audience. However, for those seeking highly coveted business positions in a discriminatory society, mastering this skill is particularly helpful.

This storytelling technique can not only be used to introduce why individuals can rightly claim a position that is normally blocked off to them, it can be used to build legitimacy and value around an individual's ideas. "[These women] build their authority in a more 360 way, so the more people that you can sell to, or the more followers you attract and the more peers, and then also the more people who are senior to you to be those gatekeepers or investors," Bowles said. "So, it's really about this narrative that people get bought into around a solution to an issue, and then [associate] you with that narrative and with the solution as the sort of identified leader around the particular change or solution that you're articulating."

By convincing others that they're the right gal for the job, these executives solidified their position as leaders of the

---

90 M. E.Heilman & Caleo, S. "Gender discrimination in the workplace," *Oxford Library of Psychology*, (2018): 73–88.

pack. Another way that these female leaders legitimized their claim to authority is to appeal to the gatekeepers' goals. It's important for aspiring business leaders to present their desires as something that is in *their bosses'* best interest. "If you're trying to negotiate something with somebody or persuade somebody, you want to look at what you're trying to get done from their perspective," Bowles said. "You want to think about why they would perceive what you're proposing is legitimate, and in their best interest."

From Bowles' research, it's clear that rhetoric can play an especially important role for those who prefer a different career trajectory and perhaps want to break free of any standard trajectory at all. The ability to craft and deliver persuasive stories is an especially powerful rhetorical tool for disadvantaged groups who can use this strategy to claim their seat at the table in the workplace.

We've covered a lot of ground in this chapter, so let's end with a quick recap. We've learned how companies use corporate rhetoric to present a more attractive view of themselves and help consumers do so as well. We also learned from Iger that for CEOs and other business leaders, knowing how to strategically label unconventional actions can help move a company forward. In the fast-paced world of acquisitions and negotiation, it's also imperative to know how to communicate clearly and directly. Bowles taught us that persuasive storytelling is a unique way women and other historically disadvantaged groups can carve out a new path for themselves. Now, armed with an understanding of several rhetorical strategies, we're ready to take a deeper dive into rhetoric.

Chapter 8

Shifting Reality

Rhetoric + Politics

Sitting among my classmates cradling our new Promethean Board egg-shaped clickers, I waited in anticipation of the results. It's 2008 and a historical presidential race is right around the corner: Barack Obama vs. John McCain. Although none of us really understood the significance of this race, the fact that it was described as "historic" lent a sense of gravity to the situation—even in our elementary school classroom. We stole furtive glances at each other as we conducted a make-believe election for president, excited to see who each of us would support if we were ten years older.

Our decision to exercise our political powers as individuals often depends on what media we consume and whether there are candidates we feel passionate enough about to support. Most citizens don't have the opportunity to get to know politicians on a personal level, so they rely on media communications (directly from a candidate or a media network) to give them a sense of who the representative is and what they stand for.

But, have you ever wondered how it's possible for the same candidate to be presented as hero or villain depending on what network you're watching? Or how the same issue can be asserted as the end of the world as we know it or the best thing that has ever happened? As it turns out, "filters," and who chooses them, are partly responsible for the diversity of perspectives audiences are presented with, particularly when it comes to politics.

Vanessa Beasley is an Associate Professor of Communication Studies at Vanderbilt University, where she is also Associate Vice Provost. Beasley's work focuses on presidential rhetoric, US political communication, and rhetorical criticism and theory. As an expert on political rhetoric, Beasley recognizes that what often appears as "straightforward" communication is often painstakingly crafted rhetoric framed in just the right way to provoke a desired response from voters. When I spoke with her, Beasley pointed out that political rhetoric is often predictable, so it's a good place to start learning how to recognize the effects rhetorical techniques can have on audiences, including yourself.

At the most basic level, learning to spot rhetorical techniques can serve as a helpful informational buffer for citizens, so they don't accept every proclaimed "truth" or policy at face value. "A citizen needs to understand by the time the message reaches you, especially through social media or television, it has been through seven or eight filters and those are really, really predictable filters," Beasley said.

While politicians may differ significantly in the amount of campaign funding or supporters they have, they all rely on the same tools, or "filters" as Beasley calls them. Filters can be any way candidates, the media, or individuals present the facts at hand. In contrast to "frames" which we'll discuss later, "filters" are chosen by the speaker to color the facts in a way that is most advantageous to them.

Imagine you're a sixteen-year-old desperate to have a car to drive to school senior year. In this case, it would be smart to use a "need" rather than a "want" filter. Presenting a car as a "back to school essential" (i.e., a need) is going to make it much harder for your parents to brush off your request as unnecessary than if you merely presented the bare facts (i.e., that a car is something that you want to have).

While this is a somewhat trivial example, politicians often employ a similar strategy: using the most favorable filter they can find to color audience members' perceptions of policies and opponents. For any given situation, there are various ways politicians can present the facts. For example, tax cuts can be presented negatively or positively depending on what filter you use. Using a filter that colors the cuts as something that saves you money will elicit a more positive response than a filter that colors it as a loss of community benefits, such as public park upkeep, that is funded by tax dollars.

While politicians choose strategic filters, it's also important to remember that the media is an important conduit through which politicians' messages reach you. While we live in an age where social media provides a powerful way for politicians to rapidly disseminate their views to the general public without going through filters they didn't choose themselves, more traditional media channels also play a powerful role in shaping political rhetoric. Oftentimes, politicians don't have control over media outlets and what filter these outlets add on. That can be a good thing, as networks are free to color situations in a way they deem fair. But, just like how a message handed off during a game of telephone becomes murkier the more times it's passed down the line, political events, messages, or policies that are filtered through various individuals and sources can become distorted. Keeping a sharp eye out for how politicians and those who disseminate their messaging filter facts is imperative to becoming a more informed citizen.

The impact of media and technology

Media channels, just like any business, know their job is to sell to the consumer. And, they know that audience members often enjoy entertaining content, even if it's not 100 percent accurate. Media channels have to sustain themselves as a business by attracting viewers, and that can include catering to a certain demographic's political views and zeroing in on who they think their viewers are, or should be.

According to the Pew Research center, 71 percent of *Wall Street Journal* readers are male and 60 percent of Fox News viewers identify as conservative.[91] Given how homogenous networks' audiences are and the media companies' desire to

---

91   Anonymous, "Section 4: Demographics and Political Views of News Audiences," *Pew Research Center - U.S. Politics & Policy*, September 27, 2012.

stimulate business, it's important to remember that politicians and their PR teams are not the only ones using filters for their messages. Media channels often apply filters that are the most favorable for them, not necessarily the politician or issue at hand.

While it may feel like politicians have finally usurped media control with the recent rise of social media, granting them the ability to directly funnel their message to millions of followers, politicians have been harnessing current technology to better persuade citizens for decades.

You might remember learning about FDR's "fireside chats," which is a great example of how presidents often incorporate new technology to more favorably present themselves to the public. In other words, new technology often gives politicians more control over their rhetoric. By 1937, 90 percent of the US population had access to a radio. This allowed President Franklin D. Roosevelt (FDR), the first president with a communications office, to speak directly to everyday Americans. FDR's famous "fireside chats" allowed him to get his messages directly to the people without the media adding their own filters first.[92] This gave FDR tremendous power to shape how citizens saw him and his policies without much outside interference, including those who may have chosen to add a filter that would negatively color an event. This invaluable ability to speak directly to the public without having his words filtered by the media in an unfavorable manner enabled FDR to maintain support during several

92 Margaret Biser, "The Fireside Chats: Roosevelt's Radio Talks," *The White House Historical Association*, August 19, 2019.

trying years in office, including handling the Great Depression and World War II.

Subsequent presidents proceeded to incorporate new rhetoric-enhancing technologies to their presidential toolkit.[93] President Dwight Eisenhower added a TV room to the White House, President John F. Kennedy incorporated TV press conferences that were broadcast live, and President Barack Obama sent the first presidential tweet. It may seem like politicians in the age of social media have a new and perhaps unfair advantage in filtering their messages and sending them out to the public with a simple tap on a screen. But, political communication, and thus rhetoric, is constantly evolving as new technology is invented and then adapted to promote their aims. "Once presidents have immediate technology in their offices, they'll never not use it," Beasley said. Regardless of political party and beliefs, "the next president after Trump will use Twitter, just use it in a different way. You can't ever put that genie back in the bottle."

Capitalizing on technology to refine political rhetoric

Robin Morgan is an American poet, author, political theorist, activist, and lecturer who has written over twenty books. Morgan highlights how technology also changes the way political candidates use rhetoric to conduct debates. She

---

93 Sean Cunningham, "A Short History of Presidential Communication," *InsideHook*, June 14, 2018.

explains how the 1948 Presidential debate had 40 to 80 million listeners who tuned in via radio broadcast that enabled more Americans to hear from the candidates themselves instead of relying on second hand news. "With each advent of radio, then television, and now social media and the Internet, the debates have changed form, content, and style," Morgan wrote.[94]

With changing technology enabling different modes of rhetorical "advertising," some politicians adjusted better than others. During the infamous 1960 Kennedy-Nixon debates, Richard Nixon refused to wear makeup and dismissed any suggestions to spiff up for the TV audience. On the other hand, John F. Kennedy paid close attention to cultivating his TV appearance, choosing to wear makeup and be particular about his wardrobe. While Nixon may have rolled his eyes at Kennedy thinking he was just being high maintenance, Kennedy was the one who got the last laugh.

Although TV debates were new to both Nixon and Kennedy, Kennedy took this new technology seriously and prepared in advance to make sure he would portray himself as the most suitable candidate. While candidates must focus on the actual content they plan on delivering, being a skilled rhetorician includes making sure you put your best foot forward in other ways too. As we'll discuss further in our chapter on law, oftentimes, especially in professions that require others to trust you, your entire aura must emanate confidence and leadership. In the end, Kennedy wowed Americans not only

---

94   Robin Morgan, "Persuasion: The Debates," *Robin Morgan*, September 27, 2020.

with his policy proposals, but a healthy dose of charm thanks to his impeccable TV appearance.[95]

While appearances certainly matter, other candidates have relied on clever rhetoric to turn a perceived weakness into a strength they have over their opponent. In a 1984 debate, Ronald Reagan (then sixty-nine years old) was facing off against former Vice President Walter Mondale (then fifty-six years old) for a second term.[96] The debate moderator for the night, Henry Trewhitt, asked the question many Americans were concerned about: was Reagan too old to be President? Trewhitt cited the many all-nighters JFK had to pull off to deal with the tense Cuban Missile Crisis and asked if Reagan could handle that level of physical (and mental) stress at his age.[97]

Reagan famously responded by turning the tables on the age question. Instead of being defensive and insisting that even as a senior citizen he was up for another term, he responded by saying, "I want you to know that also I will not make an age issue of this campaign. I am not going to exploit, for political purposes, my opponent's youth and inexperience."

Instead of accepting others' perspective of age as a disadvantage and source of concern, he framed it as an asset that he possessed and his opponent lacked. Reagan used

95   History.com Editors, "The Kennedy-Nixon Debates," *History.com*, September 21, 2010.

96   *Encyclopædia Britannica Online*, Academic ed., s.v. "Walter Mondale," last updated January 1, 2021.

97   Andrew Glass, "Reagan Recovers in Second Debate, Oct. 21, 1984,"*Politico*, October 21, 2018.

rhetoric to link youth not with strength and resilience, as we often do in our everyday lives, but with dangerous inexperience. Using witty rhetoric to address viewers' concerns, Reagan won in a landslide, pulling in 525 electoral votes, while Mondale only got thirteen votes.[98] While those who haven't studied framing and rhetoric might attribute this to Reagan's popularity, we know Reagan wasn't just skating by on charm. Reagan harnessed rhetoric to portray himself in the most favorable light possible while simultaneously suggesting why Mondale was the wrong candidate for President.

Morgan argues that because debates are filled with rhetorical strategies that enable candidates to color discussions on the merits and shortcomings of policies differently, debates are fundamental to democracy. A debate "admits to the existence of other opinions-hardly standard in authoritarian and tyrannical societies," Morgan wrote. "Persuasion may well be the only means of combining freedom and order, which is perhaps the reason that rhetoric—public speaking as persuasion—and democracy are inextricable."

Framing and priming

We've introduced the concept of "framing" in the examples above, but let's take a step back and define this key rhetorical tool. At its core, "framing" is the interpretive lens you encourage someone to view a situation through.

---

98 *Encyclopædia Britannica Online*, Academic ed., s.v. "United States Presidential Election of 1984," October 30, 2020.

For consistency's sake, let's continue on imagining what we would do if we were a high school teenager. This time, let's say that you accidentally broke your mother's favorite vase that has been passed down for generations in her family and are scared to admit it. Your clever teenage self has already gone through every possible alternative and has concluded, with a heavy heart of course, that the only viable option is to tell the truth.

In this situation, you should frame your apology as something your mom should deeply appreciate, rather than expect. This way, instead of flying off the handle, your mom will feel touched that you admitted your mistake. A way you could frame your apology, would be to say something like:

"Mom, I have something I need to confess. I was afraid to at first, but I know this is the right thing to do, because you raised me to always tell the truth, no matter how scared I am of the possible consequences. So, here it goes. I accidentally broke your heirloom vase. I know it's my fault because I was being careless when I knocked it over. I know it's not replaceable, and I'm sorry. But I'm willing to do whatever you deem necessary to make up for it."

While this may sound long-winded and unnecessary, framing the apology as something you're gathering up the courage to do prompts your mom to see it as an act that took self-sacrifice and moral strength. If you merely apologized without hinting to your mom how she should respond, it's likely she would be angry at you for breaking the vase. But, in the example above, because I've framed my apology as something I've had to struggle with, and thrown in a parenting compliment as well, I'm conveying to my mom that she shouldn't be too harsh on me because I've already repented and suffered just to get this far.

Politicians also frame their messages in a similarly advantageous way. They ponder what language and communication medium is the most effective at prompting the response they want. As we've learned, using rhetorical tools to one's advantage doesn't necessarily entail being unethical. But, as citizens who are on the receiving end of such tools, being aware that framing is a strategy used in political rhetoric safeguards you from accepting filtered and framed messages at face value.

Oftentimes, politicians will use different terms for the same topic, depending on what is most favorable for their views. One often debated topic is the idea of federal financial assistance for those in need, often referred to as "welfare." While welfare doesn't have a positive connotation, it's interesting what happens when politicians use the term "social safety net" or "assistance to people in need" instead. While all three phrases essentially refer to the same set of policies and services, according to a 2019 Pew Research study, 40 percent of Americans believe the government should do more to "provide more assistance to people in need." While party differences still exist in terms of the proportion of individuals supporting expanded aid, a more even distribution of "yeses" exist when the phrase "assistance to people in need" is used instead of "welfare." With this wording, 59 percent of Democrats support *more* assistance, while 46 percent of Republicans support *less* assistance (meaning 54 percent of Republicans supported *more* assistance, not far behind Democrats). This reveals how a simple shift in terminology can reframe an issue in a way that makes certain demographics more likely to accept or reject a concept.[99]

We're going to introduce one more tool in this chapter: priming. Beasley describes priming as "taking an existing set of attitudes that you already know exist in your audience and trying to really, really foreground them so that they become the thing that's most salient."

By priming us with topics and issues they know we care about and choosing an advantageous filter and frame, politicians are able to put rhetorical blinders on us.

When Republicans were opposing the Affordable Care Act (ACA), better known as Obamacare, one way they primed their audience to support blocking this bill was by linking increased rates of abortion to expanded healthcare access. Even though the 1976 Hyde Amendment already blocks federal funds from being used for abortion (except in cases of rape, incest, or if the woman's health is in danger), Republicans capitalized on their supporters' fear of a federal abortion mandate to garner support for opposing the ACA. By referencing abortion to conservative supporters, many of whom are anti-abortion, Republicans effectively hitched the ACA onto an issue that is already at the forefront of many conservatives' minds.[100] When such a hot-button issue is

---

99 "3. Views of the Economic System and Social Safety Net," *Pew Research Center - U.S. Politics & Policy*, December 17, 2019.

100 Caroline Kelly, "HHS Unveils New Requirement for Abortion Coverage Payments under Obamacare," *CNN*, December 20, 2019.

mentioned, it takes hold of people's minds, making it much easier for politicians to get supporters to agree that the ACA must be blocked, despite the fact that it does not provide any grounds for additional anti-abortion fears.

By clearly pointing us toward how we should not only receive their message but what prominent issues we should associate it with, politicians harness rhetoric to persuade citizens to back their campaigns, bills, and policies. Beasley references President Trump's 2020 "In Biden's America" campaign ads as an example of effective priming.[101] "The Trump campaign is assuming that their audience are people that are probably older, probably white, probably on the upper end of the socio-economic status, or lower," Beasley said. "[Regardless,] they have a fear of crime, so they're priming that fear...so that the more you watch that message, the more you think, 'Oh my gosh, I'm afraid, I'm going to do whatever it takes to keep this from happening,' and then the answer to that would be you vote for Trump."

Rhetorical twists and turns

Elected in 2016, President Trump caused quite a stir with his bold, strategic rhetoric. Since he was a candidate, Trump has been known for his confident, sweeping claims, on everything from bringing coal jobs back to how he's going to handle the national debt. In reality, Trump wasn't able to keep mines open in Arizona like he promised and has increased

---

101 Aamer Madhani, "As Crime Surges on His Watch, Trump Warns of Biden's America," *AP News*, July 29, 2020.

the national debt by \$3 trillion.[102] So, why do supporters believe his outlandish claims? An article in *The New Yorker* cites Trump's pride in his "truthful hyperbole" and how he plays to "people's fantasies."[103] These are descriptors that Trump used himself in his book, *The Art of the Deal*.

Trump also uses an "us versus them" outlook to take advantage of supporters' fears, letting it fuel support for his candidacy. By referring to him and his supporters as "us" and any opponents as ill-meaning elites (even though Trump himself is a billionaire), Trump attracted a loyal crowd of working middle-class Americans who were hungry for the power he promised he would give them. However, framing oneself as a Washington "outsider" is not a new political technique; President Jimmy Carter famously did the same in 1977.[104]

Now, let's take a quick look at the other side of the political aisle during Trump's presidency: Democrats. What tools did they use? Ralph Nader, a lawyer, advocate, and four-time presidential candidate criticized Democrats' timid language, arguing that failing to counter Republicans' claims as aggressively as they're stated is causing them to lose. "Instead of plainly saying that right-wing corporatists are lying, the mainstream media types and the Democratic Party will say it's 'magical thinking,'" Nader said in an interview with *Salon*.

---

102 Eric Lipton, "'The Coal Industry Is Back,' Trump Proclaimed. It Wasn't," *The New York Times*, October 5, 2020; Caroline Cournoyer, "Trump Promised to Eliminate the National Debt. It Has Risen by \$3 Trillion," *CBS News*, October 29, 2019.

103 Jane Mayer, "Donald Trump's Ghostwriter Tells All," *The New Yorker*, July 18, 2016.

104 History.com Editors, "Jimmy Carter," *History.com*, November 12, 2019.

"Instead of saying something is really obstructive and bad, they will substitute 'challenging.'"[105]

In contrast to Trump's bold rhetoric, Democrats chose to frame events more mildly, which signals to their supporters that "X" is not a huge deal and perhaps nothing to be concerned about.

Protecting yourself

While all this knowledge about political rhetoric may feel burdensome and a bit depressing, we are not powerless against these forces. By simply recognizing and keeping an eye out for filters, framing, and priming, you'll become more skilled in spotting when politicians are making a message, event, or fact seem like something it's not. Since these tools are used frequently in politics, it's a great place to start noticing how others use rhetoric to affect you. When you hear someone make a claim or proposal, think about how that person is framing the topic, associating it with other hot button issues (i.e., priming), and filtering it through their lens.

We also have the power of research and fact-checking. One of the best things you can do as an individual is to make sure you're getting your news from multiple reputable channels, preferably from sources with different political leanings. It's also a good idea to avoid relying on the internet for all your information. While in an ideal world all media channels would

105 Chauncey DeVega, "Ralph Nader on Trump's Corruption, 'Corporate State Fascism' and Why Democrats Keep Losing," *Salon*, October 26, 2020.

be completely unbiased, it's important to remember that every journalist, political commentator, and social media influencer is a person, and that means they are not immune to being influenced by filters, frames, and priming. As we discussed in Chapter 4, journalists are also constrained by tight deadlines that can cause some to overlook biases in their work.

It also means that, as much as they may try not to, it's possible that they unknowingly apply their own frames when conveying information to you. When browsing the internet for "news," it's important to be particularly critical of what you see; remember that anyone with decent Wi-Fi can post something on the internet, and online content often hasn't gone through the thorough framing, fact-checking, and editing process professional journalists follow.

Martin Medhurst is the Distinguished Professor of Rhetoric and Communication at Baylor University and focuses on the nature and effectiveness of political rhetoric.[106] While he believes the twenty-four hour news cycle and increased opportunities for people to share political news can boost participation numbers in democracy, he encourages citizens to not believe everything they read or see, especially online. "The thing about the Internet is that people online can maintain anonymity and there are virtually no gatekeepers," Medhurst said. "Under those conditions, you find the most extreme views being expressed by people who have no way of being held accountable."[107]

---

106 Anonymous, "Martin Medhurst," Department of Political Science | Baylor University, accessed January 20, 2021.

107 Joel Meares, "Q&A: Professor of Political Rhetoric Martin J. Medhurst," *Columbia Journalism Review*, January 10, 2011.

One of Plato's criticisms of democracy is that it relies on rhetoric, which "harms the equilibrium of the soul by appealing to one's passions."[108] Plato believed rhetoric misleads people's passions and that combining it with democracy is a toxic mix. However, because rhetoric exists and is frequently used by politicians, it's important for citizens to educate themselves and others on the various rhetorical tools politicians use to sway their passions. Being unaware of the rhetorical tools being used on us doesn't stop others from wielding them to their advantage. In summary, the best defense against political rhetoric is to arm yourself with awareness of common rhetorical tools, keep a sharp eye out for them, and conduct sufficient research from various reputable sources to piece together what the true facts are beyond various frames and filters.

Careful what you say: Rhetoric in Diplomacy

"Battling it out" probably brings to mind confrontations involving a weapon of some sort. Perhaps you picture pointed guns or bare fists colliding in the air. Luckily, unlike those featured in action movies, most real life "battles" involve more words than punches. Diplomacy, while often overlooked because it unfolds behind the scenes, is a crucial part of politics. It offers a valuable avenue whereby countries can attempt to talk things out, negotiate, and hopefully come to a peaceful conclusion without resorting to violence. When words fail, diplomacy fails, and the results can be devastating for not only individual countries but the world.

---

108 Erika Mastrorosa, "What Athenian Democracy Can Teach Us," *The Philosophical Salon*, July 16, 2020.

The US Department of State describes diplomacy as a way to promote national security while simultaneously deescalating military conflict.[109] So, with physical weapons out of the picture, diplomats rely on words to promote their country's interests. And as we've learned, whenever language is involved, so is rhetoric.

Diplomats often incorporate historical analogies into their speeches. Many of us use analogies and metaphors in our everyday lives because they give us a concrete way to describe feelings that are hard to pin down, traits that are difficult to convey, and to provide context for our comments. Calling our friend who wants to head home early from the bar "a wet blanket" or describing how "X" leader today is "so Jeffersonian" provides speakers and the audiences with common ground (often culturally based) to further the discussion. For diplomats, drawing meaningful links between past and current efforts is a way they help reinforce national narrative and identity.

The US is often described as "the land of the free" and a "champion of democracy," particularly to its citizens. Through this patriotic frame, history teachers might link US efforts in Asia and Latin America to support certain "more democratic" leaders to Americans' longstanding belief in helping revolutionaries fight for their freedom. By using rhetoric based on the nation's historical roots (i.e., the US's own revolutionary past), a teacher could convince students that modern-day military efforts in other countries reflect our history. This makes it

---

109 "About the U.S. Department of State - United States Department of State," U.S. Department of State, February 10, 2021.

easier to frame interventions abroad as righteous and even honorable, since differences between countries no longer loom as large if they share similar historical beginnings. Similarly, uniting citizens and countries behind a common historical cause is a strategy diplomats employ to their advantage.

DiploFoundation is a non-profit established by the governments of Malta and Switzerland that strives to "improve global governance and international policy development." Diplo's board members include professors of diplomacy and former ambassadors. According to Diplo, historical analogies also help make the uncertain future more digestible. "The future is always open and undetermined, and the number of international actors and the complexity of their relations are too high to give a straight clue about future developments," Drazen Pehar, an assistant professor at Keele University in the UK, wrote in an article on the Diplo website. "They indicate a direction for actions in this world, which would otherwise remain too complex to allow for an intellectual grasp. Historical analogy simply projects an image of past developments into the future and thus makes the future cognitively manageable."[110]

So, besides convincing global players to invest in a certain country's concerns and even work towards a solution due to perceived similarities in national narratives and identity, historical analogies help diplomats and politicians assuage the fears of those at home. In times of turmoil and crisis, it often helps to think you have an idea of what is going on.

---

110 Drazen Pehar, "Historical Rhetoric and Diplomacy - An Uneasy Cohabitation," *DiploFoundation*, accessed February 14, 2021.

When the COVID-19 pandemic took the world by surprise in 2020, many public figures, from doctors to journalists, referenced the 1918 "Spanish Flu."[111] Experts compared the US government's overall response to COVID-19, death toll statistics, and the economy to what happened in 1918, grasping for clues as to how the country was faring in its fight against the virus. Desperate to predict when the country could transition back to normalcy, some went even further back in history and looked at the Bubonic plague, commonly known as the "Black Death," for guidance.[112] While comparing COVID-19 to the Bubonic plague might seem like an ominous thing to do, in a modern crisis, using historical analogies referring to a disease that killed an estimated 25 million people is actually a prudent rhetorical strategy. In the midst of staggering death tolls that are mentally incomprehensible, including a similar event for audiences to compare current events to enables them to better break down what is happening in their lives.[113]

However, Pehar also warns about the disadvantages of using historical analogies in diplomacy, citing France and Britain's disastrous decision to use a strategy of appeasement to prevent war with Adolf Hitler.[114] When faced with this new, threatening opponent, French and British leaders referenced World War I, reminding their citizens that they lost about 8.5 million

111 Liz Mineo, "Harvard Expert Compares 1918 Flu, COVID-19," *Harvard Gazette*, July 21, 2020.

112 A. Shamekh, A. Mahmoodpoor, & S. Sanaie, "COVID-19: Is it the black death of the 21st century?" *Health promotion perspectives* 10, no. 3 (2020): 166–167.

113 Jenny Howard, "Plague Was One of History's Deadliest Diseases-Then We Found a Cure," *National Geographic*, July 6, 2020.

114 *Encyclopædia Britannica Online*, Academic ed., s.v. "Appeasement," accessed February 14, 2021.

lives in the last major war they participated in.[115] This historical context encouraged France and Britain to shy away from confronting the problematic annexations of countries around them. With the devastating effects of the last war as their "reference point" for the current crisis, they decided to tolerate Hitler's actions to avoid living through another world war.

Unfortunately, this historical analogy didn't prove helpful. Instead of strengthening citizens for what they had to face, it instilled fear of the unavoidable. By the time France and Britain recognized that appeasement was the wrong strategy to use, and Hitler was no regular German leader, many of their neighbors had already fallen.

While historical analogy is a helpful rhetorical tool in diplomacy, it can backfire. Having the right intentions can help, but in order to be a successful diplomat, it's also important to be wary of the possible unintended consequences of rhetorical tools, even those that are tried and true.

Another important diplomatic rhetorical skill is the ability to convey empathy for others. The Stimson Center is a research institute that works to promote "international security, shared prosperity, and justice." In a report on International Order and Conflict, P.R. Chari and Michael Newbill describe key strategies successful politicians use in diplomacy. Chari is a professor at the Institute of Peace and Conflict Studies in New Delhi and has written books on security and governance in South Asia. Newbill was the Deputy Chief of Mission (i.e.,

---

115 *Encyclopædia Britannica Online*, Academic ed., s.v. "Killed, Wounded, and Missing," accessed February 14, 2021.

the second in command in an embassy) at the US embassy in Cambodia. Focusing on diplomacy's ability to prevent countries from engaging in outright military force, Chari and Newbill emphasize the importance of using rhetoric that conveys empathy for "the other." "The other" can be an "enemy" or any country one is having tensions with.[116]

In John F. Kennedy's 1963 speech at American University, he called for a nuclear test ban. He argued for the need to achieve "genuine peace," particularly with the Soviet Union. Throughout the speech, JFK urges students to reconsider their hostility towards the Soviet Union. JFK uses rhetoric that emphasizes the Soviet Union's similarities with the US and works to break down perceived irreconcilable differences between the two countries. Kennedy describes how "among the many traits the peoples of our two countries have in common, none is stronger than our mutual abhorrence of war."[117]

Throughout his speech, Kennedy focuses on drawing connections between the US and the Soviet Union that inspire empathy rather than hostility. He even references Soviet casualties during World War II with some riveting statistics. "No nation in the history of battle ever suffered more than the Soviet Union suffered in the course of the Second World War," Kennedy said. "At least twenty million lost their lives. Countless millions of homes and farms were burned or sacked. A third of the nation's territory, including nearly

---

116 "P.R. Chari," Brookings, accessed February 22, 202; "Remarks by Deputy Chief of Mission Michael Newbill at the Combating Fake News Conference," *U.S. Embassy in Cambodia*, October 29, 2018.

117 John F. Kennedy, "Commencement Address at American University, Washington, D.C., June 10, 1963," *JFK Library*, accessed February 14, 2021.

two thirds of its industrial base, was turned into a waste-land—a loss equivalent to the devastation of this country east of Chicago."

Even in this brief excerpt from his speech, JFK uses all three rhetorical tenets (logos, ethos, and pathos) to appeal to American University seniors. Kennedy begins by drawing a historical and logical bridge between the US and the Soviet Union, emphasizing how the two countries have been allies in the past and share similar values (i.e., a loathing for war). Next, he uses statistics to appeal to ethos and pathos, suggesting that the US should feel bad for the war-devastated Soviet Union and that it's only right that we do our part to prevent another military conflict from happening. Kennedy goes even further to connect the Soviet Union to the US by citing Chicago as a mental visual aid. This brings home, quite literally, how much the Soviet Union lost during the last world conflict. And, besides helping Americans feel more open to using diplomacy over military force, by using empathy-inducing rhetoric, Kennedy is helping promote more congenial feelings towards the Soviet Union that will form a better foundation for future diplomacy. "The choice of words and re-enforcing actions can demonstrate empathy, increasing the probability of improved bilateral relations," Chari and Newbill wrote.

But oftentimes, words alone aren't enough. Being a success-ful rhetorician involves using other factors of persuasion to make your words land more effectively. Treaties and national leader meetups can be powerful symbolic tools, but in poli-tics, it helps to have some edge to your words. It's important to "combine promising words and verifiable actions."

Having the power to back up your claims and proceeding to do so helps send an even more powerful rhetorical signal to any opponents or allies. It shows that you're serious and not just spewing out empty promises. In his 1988 speech at the UN, Soviet leader Mikhail Gorbachev proclaimed that nuclear escalation is unsustainable and unwise, proclaiming that "it is obvious…that the use or threat of force no longer can or must be an instrument of foreign policy."[118]

But Gorbachev didn't just condemn weapon stockpiling. He acted on his own words and demobilized troops in the Soviet Union, signaling that he was willing to walk the talk and that other world leaders could trust him to de-escalate if they did.[119]

As a diplomatic leader, it's also important to keep in mind who your audience is. Rhetorically successful heads of state recognize that trying to be persuasive to a political opponent, versus voters at home, require different strategies. Oftentimes, leaders use aggressive rhetoric threatening military action towards foreign opponents. This is categorized as a "hard" approach. But, at home, the last thing citizens want to hear is that the country could go to war. So, leaders shift their rhetoric to appeal to their home base, adopting a "soft" approach that emphasizes peace and harmony.

While this might seem a bit manipulative, political leaders always have multifaceted challenges and goals. There are

---

118 AP, "The Gorbachev Visit; Excerpts From Speech to U.N. on Major Soviet Military Cuts," *The New York Times*, December 8, 1988.

119 F. Stephen Larrabee, "Gorbachev and the Soviet Military." *Foreign Affairs* 66, no. 5 (1988): 1002-026.

many sides to an issue, and the ability to adapt rhetorically to achieve cooperation from all parties is imperative to leaders' success and their countries'. "Carefully chosen words by national leaders can become powerful vehicles for confidence building within a broader peace-making effort," Chari and Newbill found. "Regardless of differences in nationality and political culture, the right fusion of words, symbols, and actions can resonate deeply, cutting away layers of cynicism, touching a spirit of hopefulness that lies within and isolating those who cannot budge from their grievances."

Chapter 9

Commanding
the Room

Rhetoric + Law

Have you ever been asked to "prove it?" Maybe it was a shady colleague daring you to hold him accountable for breaking professional ethics. Or, maybe it was your sibling, taunting you, knowing your parents would never believe she stole your sweater yet again. Whether used in jest or genuine challenge, most people are asked to make a case for themselves at some point in their lives. For the purposes of this chapter, when I use the phrase "make a case," I'm seeking to differentiate it from more emotional forms of persuasion. We're going to focus on rhetorical tools that are particularly helpful in situations that favor evidence and data over pathos-based arguments.

There is one industry in particular that sticks out to me when I think about making logical, evidence-based arguments: the legal field. Although some rhetorical points we'll discuss may seem obvious, keep in mind that these skills are a lot harder to put into practice and master than to simply read about. As we've seen throughout this book, often it's the tiny rhetorical shifts that most of us don't even notice that make all the difference.

Although attorneys can perform a diverse array of tasks, including writing contracts, representing clients in court, and advising companies on policy, they're hired to essentially do one thing: make sure things turn out favorably for their client. Clients can be corporations, individuals, or groups of people with a shared grievance. Because an attorney's client base can be so broad, one key skill they have to possess is how to be persuasive in any situation. That's right, attorneys are often paid thousands and sometimes millions of dollars to essentially be masters of rhetoric.

Law as rhetoric

James Boyd White is a renowned legal scholar and author of over ten academic books. Highly respected in the field, White is the L. Hart Wright Collegiate Professor Emeritus of Law at the University of Michigan, where he was also an English professor and adjunct professor of Classical Studies.[120] While it may be obvious that law is a field where rhetoric is highly relevant, to more concretely establish the relationship between the two, I want to briefly explore some of White's interpretations of law as a type of rhetoric.

---

120 "White, James Boyd - University of Michigan Law School," University of Michigan Law School, accessed February 22, 2021.

We've already discussed in prior chapters how important it is for rhetoricians to understand who they're addressing in order to craft a persuasive argument. This is also true in the legal field, whether the audience is another attorney, a judge, and/or a client. White takes this idea even further, and argues that law is "a social activity" and thus requires lawyers to be able to adjust their language to fit different cultural contexts in order to succeed. "The law can be understood as a comprehensively organized method of argument," White wrote. "It is always communal, both in the sense that it always takes place in a social context and in the sense that it is always constitutive of the community by which it works. Both the lawyer and the lawyer's audience live in a world in which their language and community are not fixed and certain but fluid, constantly remade, as their possibilities are tested."[121]

Not only do shifting cultural contexts prevent lawyers from being able to apply the same rhetoric in different situations, but the very nature of legal argument also means that lawyers have to craft new arguments, often within seconds, to address various interpretations of legal materials as they arise. White discusses how the essence of legal materials, including evidence, analogies, precedent, and statues can be constantly re-argued and re-interpreted.

This means legal rhetoric requires an additional layer of intellectual creativity that many other industries don't. Not only do lawyers have to be rhetorically aware of their own

121 James Boyd White, "Law as Rhetoric, Rhetoric as Law: The Arts of Cultural and Communal Life," *The University of Chicago Law Review* 52, no. 3 (1985): 691.

language, they have to know how to analyze others' language from different angles as well, looking for possible areas of interpretive or argumentative weakness they can exploit. "For in speaking the language of the law, the lawyer must always be ready to try to change it: to add or drop a distinction, to admit a new voice, to claim a new source of authority, and so on," White wrote. "One's performance is in this sense always argumentative."[122]

Tying this distinction back to law's infinite cultural contexts reveals why lawyers have their work cut out for them. Lawyers have to craft their rhetoric to appeal to their audience's unique culture (which may differ substantially from their own) while simultaneously re-evaluating it in real time in response to their opponent's rhetoric. This can be particularly high stakes when lawyers' entire cases hinge on a specific interpretation of a legal statute which their opponent is trying to invalidate. Similarly, when a case is banking on the successful admission of damning evidence that their opponent is trying to bar from admission, knowing how to successfully argue for its legitimacy and necessity is key.

On top of all this, lawyers have to craft coherent and convincing stories out of what evidence they have. As we'll discuss later in this chapter, lawyers are often storytellers who must create certainty out of subjective materials. "The rhetorician, like the lawyer, is engaged in a process of meaning-making and community-building of which he or she is in part the subject," White wrote. "To do this requires him or her to face and to accept the condition of radical uncertainty in which

---

122 James Boyd White, "Law as Rhetoric, Rhetoric as Law," 690.

we live: uncertainty as to the meaning of words, uncertainty as to their effect on others."[123]

With this brief overview, we're now going to delve into how, exactly, lawyers acquire such high-level rhetorical skills that are functional not only in theoretical battles with their colleagues, but when facing everyday challenges in the office or courtroom. "The knowledge out of which the rhetorician ultimately functions will not be scientific or theoretical but practical, experimental—the sense that one knows how to do things with language and with others," White wrote.

Case study: Exuding confidence and authority

Hemma Ramrattan Lomax is a US and UK qualified attorney who also has a PhD in International Law. Lomax has served in many different legal capacities throughout her career, including being a barrister (a trial attorney in the UK), law professor, advisor and representative to the United Nations, assistant parliamentary counsel, and counsel for the US Securities and Exchange Commission. Currently, Lomax is principal counsel of Global Compliance and Ethics at The Walt Disney Company.

With a resume like that, you're bound to have had to use rhetoric in various situations, even if they're all in a legal context. When I spoke with her, Lomax emphasized how refining her persuasive abilities is crucial to her success in multiple legal roles.

---

123 James Boyd White, "Law as Rhetoric, Rhetoric as Law," 695.

For lawyers, there are a few key components to building and presenting a persuasive case in any situation. Let's begin with the more "atmospheric" aspects of rhetoric first. As we've learned previously, body language can add to or take away from one's persuasiveness, and thus, rhetorical effectiveness. The main culprit that detracts from public speaking are one's hand movements. Many people like to fold their hands awkwardly in front of their abdomen or wave their hands around distractingly without any particular intention.

Getting hand motions under control, and training yourself to use them intentionally, is a key step to becoming a more persuasive speaker. Although it sounds simple, it's much harder to master than it sounds. Oftentimes, we're unaware of our body language "tics," and because awareness is the first step towards improvement, many of us have unconsciously adopted habits that detract from our rhetoric which are hard to get rid of. I've had the experience when I think I have a speech refined and memorized, only to realize when I start practicing in front of a mirror that my hand movements give off a nervous, aimless energy rather than signaling purposeful preparation as I had hoped. Luckily, there have been various studies conducted about why we move our hands when we speak that can help us get hand motions under control. For our purposes, I'll just highlight a few key takeaways.

Carol Kinsey Goman is a body language expert and author of *The Nonverbal Advantage: Secrets and Science of Body Language at Work* and *The Silent Language of Leaders*[124]. Goman

---

124 Carol Kinsey Gorman, "5 Ways Body Language Impacts Leadership Results," *Forbes*, August 26, 2018.

highlights a few key ideas everyday people can use to help refine their body language and make it more intentional. The first step is to understand the way our hand movements *should* function when we're speaking. Goman likes to think of hand motions as a second language that help reinforce verbal points in yet another way.

The way we move (or don't move) our hands, how we stand (or sit), and our facial expressions all convey a message to the audience. The tricky part is when our body language and our words don't align with or support each other. Imagine if you are saying "Our stock prices skyrocketed overnight," but instead of drawing a diagonal line upwards in the air with your hand, you drew it downwards. Despite hearing you loud and clear, your audience would be a little confused because they're receiving conflicting auditory and visual signals, both of which contribute to their understanding of what you're saying. Although your audience might know to trust your words rather than your hand gestures, unfitting or contradictory hand movements can be distracting and take away from the clarity of your message.

Lomax emphasized the importance of having a keen awareness, if not absolute control, over body language as a valuable skill to learn and have as an attorney. Lawyers are supposed to be an image of authority and refinement, so making sure external signals exude confidence is key. And, while it's not easy, learning to consistently give off an image of confidence, even if you don't feel it, is attainable with some personal reflection and practice. "If there's anything inadvertent that you're giving away by your body language, so you don't feel that confident…then you need to think about how body language can help you," Lomax said.

In the UK, barristers have worn the same style black robes and white wigs for hundreds of years. While they may seem like a silly rite of passage to becoming a barrister, they serve an important practical purpose.[125] Besides protecting barristers from being harassed if they have to represent a controversial client, they also serve as a visual equalizer that evens the playing field. "It takes away…distracting elements of persuasion," Lomax said. "So if you've got a better suit than your counterpart, maybe you'll see people assume things about you. There's a lot of assumption in communication. And so I think for persuasion, you want to clear the deck of some of the assumptions that are irrelevant to the case or the point that you're trying to make and neutralize that."

Because everyone is more or less dressed the same, barristers who know how to use body language effectively are the ones who take their persuasion to the next level. They take advantage of the clean slate provided by standardized attire to present themselves as they want to be seen. Although barristers can't rely on their wardrobe to give off a different impression than their colleagues, they can make use of their bodily cues.

Constantly double checking these outward details of your presentation may sound like a challenge that takes a while to master, and that's because it does. Recognizing the time needed to correct any distracting presentation habits and refine one's public speaking skills, Lomax and other British attorneys spend an entire year honing their presentation skills in school. They work with actors, drama teachers, and

---

125 "History of Court Dress," Courts and Tribunals Judiciary, accessed January 27, 2021.

constantly review video tapes of themselves speaking. While awareness of effective body language is a great start, even those naturally gifted at speaking need to practice to truly master this aspect of rhetoric.

As important as these nonverbal elements of rhetoric are, there are additional verbal tools attorneys have up their sleeve to amp up their persuasion. When attorneys are presenting a case in the courtroom, demonstrating that they care deeply and are passionate about the topic is a way they can exude irresistible persuasive confidence.

Imagine you've finally worked up the courage to ask your boss for a raise. If you nonchalantly mention "Oh, and I think I've done some good work and deserve a raise" at the tail end of a meeting, your boss can easily dismiss your seemingly half-hearted request. On the other hand, if you speak with an assertive tone and use the right body language when presenting ten reasons why you're indispensable to the company and should be compensated accordingly (logos), anecdotes from previous performance reviews about how respected you are for your expertise in your work (ethos), and throw in a few lines about how much you admire your boss's leadership (pathos), she is much more likely to take you seriously. More importantly, your boss is also more likely to find your arguments persuasive and request reasonable.

The same goes for attorneys when they're presenting a case in the courtroom. While many of us find it challenging to actively pay attention to a dry hour and a half office meeting, imagine how much more difficult it is for jurors to sit for hours a day, sometimes weeks on end, listening to legal evidence being presented. Because attorneys are constrained by the content they need to present and the formalities of the courtroom, they have to rely heavily on these other verbal and non-verbal rhetorical elements of persuasion to make sure their message gets across to their audience.

As much as we may wish body language, confidence, and passion are all it takes, not even attorneys can get away with relying on these techniques alone. Securing high quality content and conducting thorough research is still a necessary part of being a master rhetorician. This goes back to Cicero and Quintilian's insistence that knowledge is a precursor to successful rhetoric.

Persuasive people don't just open their mouth and "wing it," no matter how good they are at ad libbing. Lawyers often have limited time and space to get their message across, so they rely on thorough preparation to solidify what they want to convey before they even start speaking.

This may sound like a no-brainer, but it's not that easy to execute in real life. Have you ever started telling a joke and then embarrassingly forgot where it was going? Or maybe you've had the experience where you glanced at your phone in the middle of a conversation and then couldn't remember what you were talking about ten seconds previously.[126] While an occasional lapse in memory is normal and no reason for concern, these "senior moments" can be exacerbated by stress and lack of sleep. And those are two things attorneys, who

---

126 "Memory Lapse or Dementia? 5 Clues to Help Tell the Difference," Johns Hopkins Medicine, accessed January 27, 2021.

work anywhere from sixty to seventy hours a week, experience a lot.[127]

One way to fight against this natural tendency to forget what you're saying is to have a very clear picture of what your end goal is before you walk in the room. Previously conducted research and preparation is the first step to getting the basics down. "Getting what you want is not hard. It's knowing what you want. And really, I think that is core for persuasion," Lomax said. "Because how are you going to persuade anyone if you don't really know what it is you want to persuade them of? You have to look beyond the actual words."

Once you know what your core message is, it's important to convey it in a way that is engaging and captivating. In addition to capitalizing on confidence, demonstrated passion, and convincing body language, lawyers rely on storytelling to convey their point.[128] Instead of just saying "Dylan had a hard life and it caused him to make some bad choices," a lawyer would likely explain that same point in a narrative style. She would use storytelling to frame Dylan's situation as one that deserves sympathy and forgiveness. She might say something like:

"Imagine you were the only child of a single mom. A mom who loved you, but had to work three jobs to have a shot at making ends meet. Now throw in abusive boyfriends, filing in one after the other, scarring you with their violence and

---

127 Leigh McMullan Abramson, "Is There a Career in Law That Doesn't Lead to Burnout?," *The Atlantic*, September 10, 2015.

128 Jayson DeMers, "10 Presentation Tricks to Keep Your Audience Awake," *Inc.com*, August 11, 2015.

rage. Then, your mom gets sick. But there's no way to pay for her treatment because you don't have health insurance. What do you do?"

On top of a healthy dose of storytelling, lawyers often throw in the usual speaking tips.[129] This includes varying your tone to match the hills and valleys of your story, using silence to draw attention to important points, presenting your thoughts in an organized, easy to follow manner, avoiding specialized jargon, and using visual aids when possible.

Attorneys' near mastery of the verbal and nonverbal aspects of rhetoric is really what clients are paying hundreds of dollars an hour for. When people hire an attorney, it's usually because they're in a tricky situation. Attorneys are expected to swoop in and save the day, figuring out some favorable solution for their client. With a mastery of rhetorical tools under their belt, it makes it much easier for attorneys to perform well, and persuasively, under pressure.

Getting started

It can sound intimidating to strive to perfect skills that attorneys train for years to master. But mastering rhetoric is a lifelong journey anyone can begin. As much as we like to think that some people "have it" and others don't, there are steps we can take in our everyday lives to become a better rhetorician. An exercise Lomax recommends is to always

---

129 Marjorie North, "10 Tips for Improving Your Public Speaking Skills," *Harvard Division of Continuing Education Blogs*, March 17, 2020.

take responsibility for making sure what you say lands in the way you intend.

This is less of a tip and more of an actionable step centered around acknowledging that while there are various uncontrollable factors that detract from our ability to persuade someone, there are enough factors we *can* control that should enable us to succeed.

In many situations, we may not know our audiences' family background, political affinity, religious beliefs, and a host of other traits that would help us better frame and present our case. But, instead of moping about it or blaming your failure to persuade them on a lack of information, Lomax suggests reaching for your rhetorical toolkit. Using every opportunity to practice how to be more rhetorically persuasive is a way to ensure you can effectively get your point across when it really matters. The possibilities to practice this in our professional and personal lives are endless.

"So if you stand up at a meeting, you say what you think and no one's responding to you, instead of thinking, 'They don't know what I'm talking about, they don't get it,' next time, take responsibility for making sure they get it," Lomax said. "Same with your kids. Same with your husband, same with the person that you're complaining about that gives you the wrong item in your groceries. Whoever it is you're interacting with, decide to take responsibility for the message landing as you intended versus thinking it's something to do with the receiver...they may be distracted, your child might not be listening to you, [but] take responsibility. Ask yourself, how am I going to get my child to give me the attention I need to receive the message I need them to hear?"

While this sounds like quite a challenge to apply to everyday situations, it's a worthwhile one to pursue. There are many times when we would rather blame others for not understanding us, but it's unwise to neglect practicing how to get your message to land in the way you intend. If we can learn to refine our persuasive skills in relatively inconsequential matters, our rhetorical tools will be ready for us when forced to be persuasive in a situation that really counts.

When you have a message that you need to convey, you're the one "throwing the ball." Lomax uses this metaphor to emphasize how it's completely in your hands whether the ball (i.e., your idea) lands in your audiences' hands or not. How you decide to throw it, whether it's underhand, overhand, or with a triple spiral, is your choice. But, if you are throwing balls of information to your audience and they don't catch it, resist blaming it on their skills and abilities. Instead, acknowledge that you could've done better. Perhaps it's your aim, strategy, or even the type of ball you used (i.e., rhetorical method) that needs some work. Practice makes perfect, so observing what lands, what doesn't and why will take you one step closer to mastering rhetoric.

It's relatively easy to just spew out words. However, even if what is coming out of our mouth is solid content, others may not realize it unless we make it obvious. So, the next time you're dreading communicating with someone who "just doesn't get you," or trying to hold your colleagues' attention during a meeting, think back to these lawyer-approved strategies you can use: do your research, know what you want to convey before you begin speaking, project confidence, watch your body language, convince your audience that you care about the topic, and take ownership for making sure your message lands the way you want it to.

Chapter 10

Beyond the Lab Bench

———

Rhetoric + Science

In today's STEM-focused world, many claim that technical skills are the golden ticket to success. In college, the "soft" skills humanities students spend their years perfecting are often looked down upon by pre-med students and engineers. Proud of their STEM-heavy workload and constantly being told they're the "future," many of these students get away with taking no communication-related course other than their required first-year writing seminar.

However, as we've seen earlier, being a skilled communicator is an essential skill that enables doctors to more effectively assist their patients. Likewise, in the sciences more generally, it's equally important to be able to break down complex concepts, communicate how they apply to people's lives, and why they matter.

Scientists often collaborate with those outside of their immediate specialty and have business partners who have no scientific background at all. This means they need to know how to break down the minute details of their work to colleagues who aren't familiar with their field. In their paper, Cardiff University researchers H.M. Collins and Robert Evans explored how helping scientists understand the power of language through rhetorical training can help them better connect with colleagues in other fields.[130] They're not alone in their conviction of the importance of interdisciplinary research to achieve scientific excellence. In David Epstein's book *Range*, Epstein also explores the benefits of scientific collaboration and the dangers of hyper-specialization that is so prevalent in the sciences today.[131] Interdisciplinary research can help scientists discover and answer questions they otherwise wouldn't even think of. Imagine the additional challenges scientists could research and solve if they knew how to put their heads together, communicating effectively and efficiently across specialties.

Many researchers spend their career working in research labs, hoping to make discoveries that will positively impact the entire human species. But, with a general public that has at best a basic understanding of scientific concepts, convincing others why their discoveries are beneficial and safe is also a challenge. In a 2019 Pew Research survey, only 52 percent of US adults were able to identify a hypothesis, 57

---

130 H.M. Collins, and Robert Evans, "The Third Wave of Science Studies: Studies of Expertise and Experience," *Social Studies of Science* 32, no. 2 (April 2002): 235–96.

131 David Epstein, *Range: How Generalists Triumph in a Specialized World* (New York: Macmillian, 2020).

percent can correctly read a chart to answer a question prompt, and 39 percent understand that anti-acid medicine contains bases.[132]

Moreover, in recent years, there has been an increasing mistrust of previously accepted scientific innovations, such as vaccines. While some claim a religious basis for their aversion, others who oppose vaccines are simply reluctant to receive an injection of something they don't understand and do not think works.[133] Some Americans' lack of understanding and trust in science endanger society at large, allowing for the reintroduction of previously conquered diseases. While the measles were declared eradicated in the US in 2002, in 2019 there were 1,282 cases in thirty-two different states. With increasing resistance and confusion by the general public toward scientific concepts, being able to communicate the safety and practical implications of scientific work is more important than ever.[134]

Philomena Lamoureux earned her bachelor's and master's degrees in Chemistry and a PhD in Materials Science and Nanotechnology. With over ten years of computational research experience, Lamoureux is an AI scientist who specializes in machine-learning systems. Currently, she is the head of AI at Blooma.ai, a company that creates products to automate commercial real estate lending.

132 Brian Kennedy and Meg Hefferon, "What Americans Know About Science," *Pew Research Center Science & Society*, May 28, 2019.

133 Amy Boulanger, "Anti Vaxxers: Understanding Opposition to Vaccines," *Healthline*, September 15, 2017.

134 "Measles Cases and Outbreaks," *Centers for Disease Control and Prevention*, December 2, 2020.

When I spoke with her, Lamoureux emphasized that the road to becoming a better communicator is long. Particularly for professionals who didn't focus on refining their rhetoric in school, it takes a lot of hard work, determination, and practice to improve on the go. When she first began giving presentations at work, Lamoureux delved into the technicalities right from the start, expecting that those who had questions would simply raise their hand and ask for clarification. However, Lamoureux described how she didn't take into account the way company culture can discourage her colleagues, and even bosses, from asking any questions they might have. Most people, particularly those higher up on the ladder, don't want to sound uninformed or uneducated in front of colleagues.[135]

To overcome this phenomenon, Lamoureux tried explaining concepts as clearly as possible, starting from the basics and then working up to more advanced ideas. In doing so, she hoped to decrease the possibility that her colleagues had any questions at all. The fewer colleagues who left her presentation with unvoiced questions, the less confusion there was around a project, and the more successful a project was. By focusing on refining her rhetoric and making sure her message "lands" as Hemma Lomax suggested, Lamoureux was able to increase her audience's scientific understanding without tackling the greater phenomenon of self-conscious question suppression directly.

Another trick Lamoureux uses to help get her message across is to verbally prime her audience when key information is

---

135 Bill Green, "There's No Such Thing as a Stupid Question. Here's How You Can Empower Your Employees to Ask for Help," *Inc.com*, March 19, 2019.

coming up in her presentation. Doing so enables her audience to focus on what their key takeaways should be, including any actionable steps they should take afterwards. "If you go into a meeting, and you say I have an important result, then suddenly people are listening," Lamoureux said. "Because you are sort of the [messenger], you have to set the expectations of how important it is...that's why a lot of speakers when they gave a talk, they would start out with a motivation... they always start with the 'why.' Otherwise, it's not clear why you're doing this and what is it going to be used for."

Learning how to capture, retain, and guide audiences is particularly helpful for frequent presentation givers. According to an MIT Management Review, the average American worker spends six hours a week stuck in meetings.[136] The researchers only included planned meetings, so it's likely that in reality, most professionals spend an even greater amount of time in meetings. The numbers are even scarier for top executives. Senior managers tend to spend an average of twenty-three hours *per week* in meetings. That means senior managers spend about half of their work week in meetings, and over a career spanning forty-five years, this can add up to a total of twenty-two years spent in meetings.[137]

As we discussed previously, making sure you research your audience when possible is a key first step. If you're about to give a scientific presentation, this background research is

136 Steven G Rogelberg, Cliff W Scott, and John Kello, "The Science and Fiction of Meetings," *MIT Sloan Management Review* 48, no. 2 (December 2007).

137 Geoffrey James, "You Simply Won't Believe How Much Time You Waste in Meetings at Work, According to MIT," *Inc.com*, September 23, 2019.

useful, because it shapes your framing of the presentation. For example, if you find out that your audience will likely be on their fifth meeting of the day and running low on brain power, you'll know to include prominent verbal "guide marks" that highlight the most important points. Moreover, you might avoid unnecessary technical acronyms and terminology that make the concepts more complicated than they need to be. While scientific terms are fair game for those in the field, colleagues who lack the same scientific background as you (or a scientific background entirely) will easily be lost in the fray. This can cause them to tune out, missing all the important content you painstakingly planned for them.

If someone begins a slide with, "This section details how we can use our latest discovery to create a new immunotherapy drug that will make billions of dollars and save millions of lives," I know my ears would perk up immediately; I'd be engaged and excited to find out how we're going to use our research to take cancer treatment to a new level. Now, imagine if that same presenter opened with this instead:

"Today we're going to explore how our research into various immune system checkpoints, including those suppressed by drugs like Pembrolizumab that target PD-1, could potentially lead us to an exciting new drug that would inhibit another common immune-suppressive pathway."

While some may be able to follow along, this second opening doesn't grab the audience's attention as effectively. For one, it overloads the audience with technical jargon and the chemical names of specific drugs. While interesting and important for a scientist to know, including such detailed information is unnecessary and confusing for a general audience. It can also alienate them, decreasing their desire to try to understand something so clearly out of their expertise.[138] Moreover, this opening uses several qualifying, but vague words like "could" and "potentially" that can cause people to tune out, assuming the information being presented isn't really that groundbreaking.

In contrast, the first opening cuts to the chase as to why audience members should even pay attention to the presentation. It makes it clear that this is exciting science that will generate impressive financial returns and impact millions of lives. As a result, the first opening allows listeners to better focus their energy on understanding the data that is about to be presented, and, perhaps more importantly, its implications.

Achieving engaging clarity

Learning how to break down complex concepts into clear, digestible pieces, especially to those outside a particular scientific field, takes years of practice. In order for scientists to practice with realistic audience members, they have to get out of their industry bubble. Presenting to colleagues in the same field who understand the findings you're presenting by heart won't provide accurate feedback about the clarity of your presentation. As scientists who are so intrigued by the topic that they're also devoting their lives to studying it, close colleagues won't be much help in gauging how engaging

---

138 Andrew H Hales and Kipling D Williams, "Alienating the Audience: How Abbreviations Hamper Scientific Communication," *Association for Psychological Science*, January 31, 2017.

your presentation is either. "I think people in technical fields, especially PhD types, are really used to working on their own and being self-starters and learning it all by themselves," Lamoureux said. "And it's really hard to put yourself into the mind of someone who doesn't know your knowledge. So you think you're breaking it down, you think you're making it simple, but in the end you can only understand if that is actually the case if you talk to someone else."

Lamoureux suggests calling up your friends and family who are not fellow scientists, or specialists in the same field, and trying to explain a complicated concept to them. By practicing how to introduce and explain scientific theories and findings with others, scientists can learn to what extent they have to go over what they consider are "the basics." Practicing in everyday conversations can also provide scientists with pointers on how to keep their audience engaged.

If you're someone with a non-technical background, one way you can help your scientific colleagues learn to become better communicators and refine their rhetoric is to speak up when you don't understand something. While it takes courage to be the first to say "I have no idea what you're talking about," no one is a mind reader, so feedback is extremely important. By speaking up, you'll help save colleagues from years of ineffective presentations, and kick start their journey to becoming a master rhetorician.

Bob Dignen has taught Business English in the UK for over ten years and helps train leaders to be better communicators. Dignen emphasizes how questions from colleagues help notify leaders of their areas of improvement and enables them to learn from their mistakes. While scientists should proactively practice with those in different fields to learn how to take things apart and communicate them clearly, those with non-technical backgrounds play an important role in helping jumpstart their scientific colleagues' rhetorical journeys.[139]

With science already at the forefront of moving humanity forward and improving people's quality of life, it's exciting to think about how much faster human progress could be if those with technical backgrounds focused more on refining their rhetoric.[140] Moreover, with new technologies all over the media, having a strong grasp on rhetoric can be particularly helpful for scientists trying to assuage misinformed fears. "Good communication can really be useful because you can really convince people of your social mission, [and with that] you can take people's fears away," Lamoureux said. "So it's a tool with which you can do a lot of good in the world."

Funding scientific careers

When we think of "scientists," we often envision someone in a white lab coat and protective goggles, holding a test tube or pipette. What most people don't envision is someone writing for hours each day, working on a career-changing paper.

139 Bob Dignen, "Five Reasons Why Feedback May Be the Most Important Skill," *Cambridge University Press*, March 17, 2014.

140 Valentí Rull, "The most important application of science: As scientists have to justify research funding with potential social benefits, they may well add education to the list," *EMBO reports* no. 15 (2014): 919-22.

While the idea of "science" more generally doesn't have communication with others (i.e., patients, the general public) as clearly built into its backbone as medicine, rhetoric still plays an essential role in scientists' success. Some scientists may be more involved in the business world like Lamoureux, frequently giving presentations and making use of oral rhetoric, while research-based lab scientists communicate their findings more frequently through written rhetoric.

However, one key, and perhaps dreaded, part of being a scientist is the need to secure grants. This never-ending cycle of writing grant proposals and getting them approved is sometimes a surprise to students who thought they'd be spending most of their time designing and conducting experiments at the lab bench. However, as unwelcome as it may be, writing grants is not only a part of the job, but what creates the job.

Even though scientists may start out with a shakier rhetorical foundation than their humanities-trained colleagues, it's never too late to begin learning to master rhetoric. A key to successful grants is to clearly and convincingly outline why "X" proposed research idea is novel and worth spending thousands, if not millions of dollars on. Essentially, a grant proposal details the questions a scientist is hoping to answer, how this novel question builds upon previous scientific research, outlines how an experiment will run, and how the funds will be spent (if provided). Moreover, a grant proposal needs to successfully convince a panel of scientific critics that a question is not only unique enough to investigate for the sake of intellectual curiosity, but has powerful potential applications that will benefit society. That is quite a tough question to answer in a succinct proposal.[141]

In a field that particularly appreciates concise writing, a strong grasp on rhetoric will enable some scientists to out-write, and thus out-fund, other labs. And, it'll enable them to better persuade their audience, often top scientists in their field.

Without funding, no matter how driven and bright scientists are, they won't be able to carry out their experiments. Even though it's integrated into scientists' career, grant writing is stressful and has high stakes. To put things into perspective, an Australian study on grants revealed that out of 3,727 proposals, only 3,570 were reviewed. Out of those 3,570 proposals, only 731 proposals received funding (a 21 percent "acceptance rate").[142]

In addition to pressure caused by the relatively low probability of having a grant proposal accepted, this study found that it takes researchers an average of thirty-four working days to write one proposal. Even though most scientists work longer hours, assuming a grant-writing scientist works nine to five, that adds up to a total of 272 hours of writing. In reality, it can take even longer to finish up if researchers have to re-submit their proposals for a second review. While an intuitive solution might be to go above and beyond, writing,

---

141 Anonymous, "Proposal Writing," Northwestern University Office of Undergraduate Research, accessed January 28, 2021.

142 Danielle L Herbert et al., "On the Time Spent Preparing Grant Proposals: an Observational Study of Australian Researchers," *BMJ Open*, no. 3 (2013).

re-writing, and editing a proposal to increase the chances it'll be approved, unfortunately, increasing the time spent on a proposal did not lead to increased chances of acceptance.

As you can imagine, being under financial pressure to not only fund your salary but other team members' in the lab can be stressful. For scientists passionate about their research, securing enough grants is not only a means of funding their career, but their life purpose. Those who are Principal Investigators, or heads of their own lab, also have the pressure of obtaining enough funding to keep their entire team employed. In order to meet grant deadlines on top of completing their everyday research responsibilities, many scientists sacrifice time with family and friends. In a survey conducted by *The Guardian*, 93 percent of researchers said they're stressed by applications generally and 83 percent said they decreased vacation time during grant-writing season.[143]

Between 2014-2020, the European Union's largest research program to date (The European Commission's Horizon 2020 Programme) provided $89 billion of funding. The commission reported a 14 percent success rate for proposals.[144] That's about the same admissions rate as being accepted into a top twenty-five US university. This means that scientists who don't have a strong grasp on rhetoric stand to lose millions of dollars in funding that could've gone towards their research and livelihood.

---

143 Adrian Barnette and Danielle Herbert, "The Personal Cost of Applying for Research Grants," *The Guardian*, April 7, 2014.

144 Emily Sohn, "Secrets to Writing a Winning Grant," *Nature News*, December 20, 2019.

As we're starting to see, regardless of whether professionals enjoyed writing in school and worked to refine it in their youth, it has a way of resurfacing in every profession. Particularly for scientists whose formal education didn't require extensive rhetorical training, neglecting to attend to their rhetorical education heightens their everyday stress on the job.

How can scientists become better writers?

Because learning to master rhetoric is a lifelong journey, constant practice is one of the most helpful steps scientists can take to improve their chances of success. Constantly writing and submitting proposals can be discouraging but it is an inevitable part of being a researcher. Even being a Nobel Prize winning scientist doesn't ensure grant approval. In fact, on the day molecular biologist Carol Greider won the Nobel Prize in 2009, she was notified of a rejected grant proposal.[145]

Luckily, scientists can make use of some simple rhetorical tips to begin refining their rhetoric. Behavioral scientist Kylie Ball has received more than $25 million in grant funding but encourages fellow scientists not to be discouraged. In an interview with renowned scientific journal *Nature*, Ball admits that while she's had over sixty grants funded, she's "also had probably twice as many rejected."[146]

A grant-writing veteran, Ball advises researchers to know their audience. Sound familiar? Ball is essentially suggesting

---

145 Ibid.
146 Ibid.

what Vanessa Beasley, Victor Wu, Hemma Lomax, and Aristotle have all confirmed: you need to investigate and understand your audience in order to make a persuasive argument for what you want.

Conducting background research beforehand so they know what their panel is looking for can save scientists a month plus of work writing a proposal that is not a good fit for what their audience is looking for. Sometimes rejection isn't personal, it's a matter of suitability. If scientists pay careful attention to what their target audience likes and what they're hinting they prefer via a revision request, it's much more likely the proposal will be approved.

Cheryl Smythe, an international grants manager at the Babraham Institute in the UK, also stresses the importance of writing with your audience in mind. "Imagine you're tired, grumpy and hungry. You've got fifty applications to get through," Smythe said. "Think about how you as an applicant can make it as easy as possible for them."[147]

Scientists need to write in a way that will persuade their audience. This includes attending to their unique backgrounds, research interests, and past papers, among other considerations in their proposals. Smythe also advises scientists to avoid convoluted or confusing sentences and to make sure that font and formatting don't distract from the content.

Taking the time to understand your audience and keeping them in mind when writing grants can be the difference between a few million dollars' worth of funding and zero.

---

147 Ibid.

Case Study: Effectively communicating with the general public

While not every scientist is passionate about communicating their knowledge to the public, some consider it part of their scientific calling. Neil deGrasse Tyson is an astrophysicist who has been the director of the Hayden Planetarium in New York City since 1996. Tyson studied at Harvard, the University of Texas at Austin, and Columbia University, and is widely acknowledged as a skilled scientific communicator. He is an author, regular guest on Stephen Colbert's *Late Show*, has a YouTube channel called "StarTalk," has narrated science documentaries, and even made a guest appearance on *The Big Bang Theory*.[148]

As a seasoned scientific communicator, Tyson has developed an impressive rhetorical guidebook to teach the general public complex scientific topics. One of his top tips is preparation, including shaping his rhetoric to fit different types of media. For example, TV requires visual and body language preparation, while a podcast might not. Regardless of the medium of communication, ensuring a clear presentation requires extensive rhetorical preparation. "You need to be ten times more prepared than anything you might invoke in order to look like you didn't prepare at all," Tyson said. "The same ideas, the same concepts can be framed, shaped, in different ways depending on the audience. Depending on what makes that audience tick, relative to this audience."[149]

---

148 "Home," Neil deGrasse Tyson, accessed January 28, 2021.
149 Neil deGrasse Tyson, "Communication: It's Not Enough to Be Right," Neil deGrasse Tyson Teaches Scientific Thinking and Communication, November 13, 2020, MasterClass video, 4:30.

Part of preparation is keeping his audience in mind. A science documentary's audience may differ from those watching a late-night talk show or his YouTube channel. Tyson stresses that if scientists neglect to shape their message to fit their specific audience, they won't be able to effectively communicate their message. "If you're going to tell anybody anything, either an individual, a small group, a large group…you have to understand your audience," Tyson said. "You have to. Otherwise, it's two ships passing in the night. Otherwise, you'll be lecturing and not communicating."[150]

In order to ensure his message is tailored to a specific audience and is digestible, Tyson likes to do what Lamoureux does: grab a friend to gather critical feedback. If no one's available, he spends some time writing down exactly what he plans to say, so he can take a critical look at it himself. "Ninety percent of the sentences that come out of my mouth publicly have been previously written down," Tyson said. "They existed in written form before they come out of my mouth. It allows you to organize your thoughts without someone judging it in that instant. It gives you a chance to rework an idea and show it to someone else: 'Is this clear to you?'"[151]

To strengthen and refine his ability to communicate clearly and effectively, Tyson recommends being an avid reader of high-quality literature. There's a saying that says if you want to be a good writer, you have to be a good reader first. Tyson's experiences confirm this; like advertising expert Jeff Goodby, Tyson believes reading literature helps people learn how to

150 Neil deGrasse Tyson, "Preparing for Your Audience," 0.01.
151 Neil deGrasse Tyson, "Preparing for Your Audience," 10:26.

use language better and introduces them to the varied ways they can use language more generally.

Tyson is also a fan of using humor to keep his audience engaged, as well as using helpful hand gestures to emphasize his main points. As a former dancer, Tyson takes advantage of his confidence and familiarity with his body to communicate more effectively. "Spoken word can do a really good job. But you're not limited to that," Tyson said. "Why not allow your body to participate in the act of communicating? It'll double your effectiveness."[152]

As a scientific communicator constantly engaging with the public, Tyson also has some tips on how to engage in scientific discourse with those who are skeptical of science. The first step is to listen, not judge. In order to prepare your answer, you need to understand your audience. This begins with genuinely listening to what your colleagues' concerns, doubts, and confusions are. "I've had encounters with people and they'll say things like, 'Just tell them they're wrong,' and it's like no," Tyson said. "Because that's not going to work. I'll be right, but it's not effective. If I'm going to be effective, I need to know in advance, how are they thinking, how is their brain wired, what biases are they most susceptible to…so that I can say 'here is information I can fit in this way,' maximizing the chance they can say 'I've never thought about it that way.'"[153]

While your colleague is voicing their concerns, you can begin thinking about how you're going to respond. Focusing on

---

152 Neil deGrasse Tyson, "Communication Tactics," 10:32.
153 Neil deGrasse Tyson, "Communication: It's Not Enough to Be Right," 5:06.

how you're going to frame your explanation or argument to match your specific audience's concerns will give you the highest chance of communicative success. Asking follow-up questions to gain additional clarity on why your audience has specific questions or doubts is also a powerful tool. Their responses might reveal something about their background, way of thinking, or personal challenges that are deterring them from a specific scientific concept or innovation.

Preparing future scientists to succeed

In a research article on scientific literacy, associate professor in the rhetoric and writing studies program at Western Michigan University Maria Gigante describes how "future scientists are not learning how arguments are structured, meaning is made, and facts are agreed upon—specifically through communicative practices—both within and outside of the scientific community." This gap is not only an inconvenience to scientists themselves but also a potential barrier to successfully bringing valuable scientific information to the general public whose tax dollars fund a significant portion of scientific research.

If scientists make important discoveries that have huge potential societal impacts but can't communicate why they're important and get government officials and the general public on board, it's a loss for all of us. Not only will scientists be frustrated that they've wasted years of time, effort, and resources on something that won't be applied or implemented, the public could be missing out on new discoveries that hold powerful benefits.

To prevent such a catastrophe, future scientists should be trained in scientific communication alongside their biology and physics courses. "A science writing and communication course that is grounded in the rhetoric of science and that also has sociological, philosophical, and historical components can provide science students with a critical awareness of how their discipline operates in society and teach them how to become more responsible and effective communicators," Gigante wrote.[154]

Incorporating rhetoric courses into science curriculums is a powerful way for schools to better prepare future researchers for success. In fact, some scientists consider being able to communicate with the general public and lawmakers a key part of their careers.[155] Far from being on the sidelines, rhetoric is at the forefront of a successful career in the sciences.

Scientists like Lamoureux and Tyson have shared how they constantly practice communication to refine their rhetorical skills. But they would've had a head start professionally if they had a more rigorous rhetorical curriculum in their formal education. Some schools have recognized this gap between understanding science and being able to communicate what you know. To address this need to bridge the gap between possessing technical knowledge and knowing how to communicate it, several colleges have relatively new

---

154 Maria E. Gigante, "Critical Science Literacy for Science Majors: Introducing Future Scientists to the Communicative Arts," *Bulletin of Science, Technology & Society* 34, no. 3–4 (June 2014): 77–86.

155 Michael L. Pace et al., "Communicating with the Public: Opportunities and Rewards for Individual Ecologists," *The Ecological Society of America* 8, no. 6 (August 1, 2010).

majors aimed at training students to communicate scientific and technological topics specifically.[156]

While communication in science and technology majors may not be able to write grant proposals or possess in-depth scientific knowledge, their ability to communicate complex concepts in terms everyday people can read and understand opens up doors closed to many "traditional" scientists who aren't as skilled communicators. The career options open to skilled scientific communicators include becoming a journalist, medical writer, freelance writer, and general scientific publications writer.[157] Those skilled in scientific communication have an astounding 49,350 job results to choose from on LinkedIn, including becoming Director of Communications for companies and department heads at universities.[158]

Many people go into the sciences because they want to make discoveries that change the world as we know it. Discoveries that will move humanity forward, help those around them, and create a better world for future generations. In order to assist current and future scientists on this honorable mission, schools should place a greater emphasis on rhetoric. Scientists must also strive to communicate clearly, collaboratively, and persuasively.

---

156 "Best Colleges with Technical and Scientific Communication Degrees," *Universities.com*, accessed February 22, 2021.

157 "Science Communication and Outreach Careers," University of California San Francisco: Office of Career and Professional Development, accessed February 22, 2021.

158 "Science Communication in the United States: 49,350 Results," LinkedIn, February 22, 2021.

Chapter 11

Keeping Up with the Hustle

Rhetoric + Entertainment

You yawn, and then glance at your watch. Seeing that it's 11:35 p.m. ET, wakes you up with excitement and you get ready to settle down on the couch with an evening drink. On weeknights, millions of Americans tune into their favorite late-night talk shows in a similar manner. From Trevor Noah in NYC to Jimmy Kimmel in Hollywood, late-night hosts play an important role in helping audiences process serious current events with lighthearted monologues. They also provide the public with their weekly dose of celebrity interviews, and even produce their own mini musical performances. An average of 3.1 million viewers tune in to the top rated *Late Show with Stephen Colbert* on CBS, which provides a snapshot of the large audience talk show hosts have direct access to.[159] With so

---

159 John Koblin, "Stephen Colbert Signs a New 'Late Show' Deal Through 2023," *The New York Times*, October 17, 2019.

many people listening to every word they say, hosts are under tremendous pressure to balance being fresh and comedic, with addressing heartbreaking news as needed.

Most late-night shows air live four to five times a week, and with the twenty-four-hour news cycle and social media always churning out more "breaking news," consistently producing high-quality shows is no easy task.[160] As we learned from Tom Lee in our chapter on journalism, there's a lot that goes into the media before it's released to the public. To get everything done, these entertainers rely on dozens of dedicated staff members who work tirelessly to script the show, write jokes, fact-check monologues, put together news clips, book clients, and a variety of other tasks that keep the program running like clockwork. For most shows, there are over twenty writers alone on staff.[161]

Working in the media industry, those in entertainment rely heavily on communication and skilled rhetoric to succeed. Communication is not only an essential aspect of the industry, but also a key part of employees' everyday lives. Whether it's getting their foot in the door by convincing hiring managers they have something special to offer or frantically coordinating with colleagues to put together a show that will air on national television within a matter of hours, being a strong communicator is a prerequisite to success in the field.

160 Liane Hansen and David Folkenflik, "The Power of the 24-Hour News Cycle," *NPR*, May 29, 2005.

161 Rebecca Alter, "A Guide to Every Writers' Room on Late-Night TV," *Vulture*, March 20, 2020.

Working in entertainment often means being part of a media company. Media companies sustain themselves by persuading viewers to choose their TV shows, anchors, news coverage, and streaming services over their competitors. So, being skilled at written and oral rhetoric in order to conduct everyday internal operations and effectively convince audiences to commit to "X" show is the bedrock of entertainment. Now that we have a brief overview of some of the communicative and persuasive challenges those in entertainment face, let's dive into some specific examples of how understanding rhetoric helps professionals succeed in this highly competitive field.

Case Study: Communicating with colleagues in the film industry

Hans Zimmer is a German composer of major film scores including *The Lion King, Gladiator, Inception,* and *Interstellar.* He's earned Academy awards, Tony awards, Grammy awards, and the Lifetime Achievement Award in Film Composition from the National Board of Review, among other prestigious acknowledgements.[162]

As a composer, Zimmer doesn't get paid for his words. But, he is hired to tell stories through music, and works closely with directors and actors to nudge an audience member to feel despair, joy, anticipation, and other complex emotions. A frequent colleague of other industry stars, Zimmer has learned some rhetorical tools that enable him to effectively

---

162 "Hans Zimmer," IMBD, accessed January 31, 2021.

communicate his vision and perspective on films with his colleagues who don't have a background in music.

One of his tips is to distill requests into the most simplistic language possible. As AI scientist Philomena Lamoureux emphasized, getting into technical weeds is a rhetorical trap specialists should avoid. As a talented and experienced composer, it can be tempting to use a plethora of complex musical terms when discussing music-related matters with colleagues. But, Zimmer has learned that as much as he may enjoy such a musically rigorous conversation, such technicalities get in the way of clear instructions. Without precise rhetoric, others aren't able to understand his concerns and revisions, which delays the whole film making process. "Speak in plain English," Zimmer said. "It's what they teach you as a kid. Use your words and don't get technical. Don't make it into a technical conversation."[163]

While there are cases where technical terms are helpful, such as in conversation with other composers, the conductor, or musical colleagues, when communicating with directors focused on high-level aspects of the work, less is more. "Don't have the conversation where you get nerdy...I can get all carried away and it has nothing to do with anything," Zimmer said. "Stop being technical, stop being scientific, communicate to them in the simplest possible way."[164]

In film, communication is critical to developing a coherent, complex, and enthralling story that the audience can enjoy.

---

163 Hans Zimmer, "Directors: Part 2" in Hans Zimmer Teaches Film Scoring, January 21, 2021, MasterClass video, 2:13.

164 Hans Zimmer, "Directors: Part 2," 2:41.

There are hundreds of moving parts in a film, including everything from getting the actors to portray the character you envisioned in your mind, to making sure the lighting supports a scene, to ensuring actors' wardrobe adds to the story. Making sure a film's score supports and doesn't distract from the style and message of the movie is essential. Zimmer describes how he works closely with directors, communicating back and forth to ensure their visions for the film, and opinions on what the film lacks, align. "I work really hard at trying to understand and have conversations about what this movie is about," Zimmer said.[165]

Otherwise, unintentionally conflicting messages and storytelling that confuse the audience may sneak into the final cut. Just like how body language that doesn't match one's words is distracting to audience members in a presentation, having different aspects of the same film conflict makes the audience pause—and not in a good way.

As one of the key leaders in producing a film, Zimmer not only has to coordinate with the director, but communicate his artistic vision to the musicians playing his score. This includes making sure musicians know why they're playing each note and how each note contributes to the story. Everyone has to be on the same page, and it's part of Zimmer's responsibility to make sure his team is working under the same vision.

Because creative endeavors are often abstract and complicated, even entertainers whose primary contributions aren't

---

165 Hans Zimmer, "Directors: Part 1," 1:51.

directly related to language can't escape the importance of rhetoric and communication in their career. Recognizing this, Zimmer has worked to refine his communication skills over the years, even though it didn't come as naturally to him as music.

Case Study: Connecting with viewers

Robin Roberts has been an anchor on ABC's *Good Morning America* (GMA) for fifteen years and in the broadcasting industry for over thirty years. Under her leadership, Roberts has helped GMA win four Emmy awards for Outstanding Morning Program and has received numerous individual awards for her work.

As a journalist, Roberts relies on rhetoric and communication every day at work. Through her professional experiences, Roberts has gathered an impressive set of rhetorical tools that help her authentically communicate with others. However, Roberts emphasizes that being a skilled, authentic communicator is a skill everyone, not just journalists or public communicators, need to succeed in their lives. "I can't think of any line of work, anything that you're doing that you are not going to benefit greatly by being able to communicate effectively," Roberts said. "Nothing is going to get you farther along than being able to communicate and connect with people."[166]

---

166 Robin Roberts, "Meet Your Instructor," in Robin Roberts Teaches Effective and Authentic Communication, October 1, 2020, MasterClass video, 3:07.

As a broadcast journalist, Roberts built a fan base centered around herself. Her viewers are choosing to tune in to not just "the news" but "the news with Robin Roberts." So, central to her professional success is being able to consistently present a genuine, authentic image that viewers feel they can relate to.

As we've explored, there's no causation between *intending* to convey something and successfully conveying it. Roberts often interviews others, during which she is not doing a lot of talking but listening. Many interviewees talk about sensitive subjects and are trusting Roberts enough to open up to her (versus another journalist). When navigating conversations filled with vulnerability, Roberts suggests using body language to demonstrate you're an active listener.

Conveying your interest in others while you are *not* speaking eliminates many of the rhetorical techniques we've learned so far. But body language and other nonverbal cues can be just as powerful in encouraging others to tell their story. Oftentimes, Roberts visibly leans forward in her chair when asking an interviewee a question. While this may be a natural, almost reflexive response for those interested in what someone else is saying, this is a nonverbal rhetorical strategy that is useful in various contexts. If you're sitting in a meeting or grabbing coffee with a client, one way you can effortlessly demonstrate your genuine concern and interest is to lean forward as if you need to be closer to hear what they're saying.

The second part of conveying genuine interest in an interviewee is to make sure you tell their story effectively. In order to convey not just the dry facts, but the story behind the facts, Roberts relies on two skills various professionals have highlighted: understanding her audience and doing her homework.

Before she even attempts to convey a news story, Roberts makes sure she is clear about what the message behind the facts is and how she can best relay this to the American public. This can include considering the climax of a story, what background information is most relevant, and what the key takeaways should be for the general public. "People don't really care too much about facts, but if you can get the message across through a story, especially through a personal story you have, that's very effective," Roberts said.[167]

Another strategy Roberts uses is to vary her tone to match the gravity of the situation she's reporting. Much like how a lawyer would be careful to not sound too upbeat about a tragic murder or too downcast about a client's positive contributions to the community, Roberts makes sure her tone matches the story. Taking advantage of this aspect of rhetoric, Roberts cues listeners in on what type of content she's about to present and assists their thought process. "Let your voice reflect the tone of the story," Roberts said. "It helps [the audience] have a better understanding of what the subject is, what they're about to see or what they're hearing, and help them understand the story."[168]

While storytelling can help keep an audience engaged, news anchors also need to keep their audience's attention span in

---

167 Robin Roberts, "Public Speaking," 1:17.
168 Robin Roberts, "Behind-the-Scenes at Good Morning America," 5:12

mind. When people hear a list of unfortunate events in a row, it's easy to tune out and lose track of what you're supposed to be understanding. Roberts worked hard to refine her ability to not "chase rabbits," going in circles before getting to the point of the story. "You need to be more concise in what you're saying...keep it simple," Roberts said. "That's what I do when I find I'm not connecting."[169]

These seemingly simple tips, a mix of verbal and nonverbal rhetorical tools, is what Roberts has relied on for decades to lead her co-anchors and team members to broadcast journalism success. As simple as these rhetorical skills are on paper, Roberts has learned and refined them over years of practice. In fact, for many of her tips, such as how to avoid "chasing rabbits," Roberts is still in the process of mastering them. It just goes to show that if an award-winning news anchor still needs to refine her rhetoric, mastering it is indeed a lifelong journey.

We've covered a lot in this chapter, including how important it is to proactively consider the connotations and nuances of one's messaging. Whether it's in scripted jokes, monologues, or one's day-to-day communication with colleagues, taking the time to think about the impact language can have saves entertainers a lot of trouble (and money) down the line. Moreover, we've learned that entertainment is a collaborative field with directors, makeup artists, dialogue coaches, and the film crew, among others, working together to create a beautiful story for the audience. Because so many parties are involved, coordination is key. In order to coordinate

---

169 Robin Roberts, "Public Speaking," 4:47.

these moving parts, entertainers have to have strong rhetorical skills.

As a practical exercise, the next time you make a mistake, remember how entertainment professionals use rhetoric to keep the ball rolling without stepping on any toes along the way. Be direct and concise with your thanks and apologies. By clearing out any areas of contention or conflict as soon as possible, you can make sure your communication channels stay clear and open, which you'll need to prepare for tomorrow's show.

Chapter 12

Putting Your Best Foot Forward

Rhetoric + Organizational Effectiveness

We've learned a lot about the art of speaking, presentation, and writing, but one cannot employ skilled rhetoric without knowing how to first listen to others. As we've seen, in order to effectively frame situations, proposals, and requests in a favorable way, you first have to know your audience. "Knowing" entails understanding what motivates your audience and having as much background information on them as possible. The reason for this is simple: it's hard to pitch an idea to someone in a way they'll likely accept if you don't know what makes them tick.

While rhetoric is the art of being persuasive in any situation, meaning with any audience, most of the time speakers know the demographics of their target audience and shape their message appropriately.

In school, depending on the grade level and subject, I noticed how teachers would emphasize different aspects of a topic and their personality. Some relied on their comedic, playful side to keep students entertained. I had a sixth-grade history teacher who would periodically invite "guest speakers" from history (Caesar and Confucius are two I remember) who were really just him dressed up in some ridiculous costume quoting ancient writings. While this sounds silly looking back, I absolutely loved it when I was eleven. This is a great example of a teacher who understood his audience and played up certain aspects of his personality to effectively convey his message. At the time, I thought my teacher's aim was pure entertainment, but now I can see I underestimated him. By keeping students laughing, he succeeded in making history "fun," which accomplished his goal as a teacher.

In contrast, as I grew older, teachers changed their teaching approach. My high school teachers often took their time getting a feel for each class, observing students' personalities and priorities before choosing an appropriate rhetorical method for their teaching. Some sensed students' fear of getting into "good" colleges like a shark smelling blood in the water and promptly capitalized on it to motivate students to push themselves academically. Others sensed that same fear and anxiety but decided a lax, "do what works for you" approach would be more effective.

Regardless of their varying teaching styles and audience members, these teachers all had one thing in common: they listened. They listened to students' outbursts, frustrations, and what they excitedly chatted about before class started. By listening first, teachers were able to pinpoint their audience's motivators, fears, and quirks. This enabled them to choose the most effective rhetorical approach when speaking with individual students or the class as a whole.

Presenting feedback effectively

Do you remember Jeff Goodby and Rich Silverstein from our chapter on advertising? As the co-partners of their firm, they're the top bosses. And, as much as managers enjoy praising employees for their hard work, they're also responsible for providing critical feedback. Negative feedback can sometimes feel deeply personal, so in order to establish an effective critique culture, managers need to pay close attention to each employee's personality. Personality affects how someone reacts and enable managers to better frame their feedback in a way that will likely be helpful instead of hurtful. "It's an important thing to kind of scope out the personality of the person you're dealing with so you can kind of know what it means when he or she says this," Jeff Goodby said. "Different people you treat differently. There are some people you know who can take it, that you can just be really direct with them, you can joke with them and tell them it sucks...there are some other people where if you stop them halfway through the script, they want to jump off the bridge."[170]

---

170 Jeff Goodby and Rich Silverstein, "On Craft: Writing, Design, and Giving Direction," 7:16.

So, how do managers learn the varied personalities of their staff? By listening and observing how they tend to react in different situations. Being a good listener on an everyday basis enables managers to have the background knowledge necessary in order to provide the most strategic feedback possible. Being careful to offer reasons behind a critique is also important and can take the edge off a conversation for more sensitive types. "You don't have to have an opinion on the spot. You have to find a way to have the conversation continue so they don't just break down," Goodby said. "Because creative people are sensitive. They're sensitive to your body language, they're sensitive to the way you say things, they're tuned in on every word, so you have to be careful."[171]

Something else that can help is to present feedback in a psychologically safe environment. Some employees are less easily embarrassed in front of their colleagues, while others may feel self-conscious even when presenting their best work. One way to avoid creating a culture of fear around feedback is to help shape employees' projects privately and then providing an opportunity for them to share their work once it's achieved a certain standard. "I don't like to have people give their ideas in front of other people until we're pretty far down the road and everyone's got something good and worked out...if you're killing ideas in front of other people it's really demoralizing."[172]

---

171 Jeff Goodby and Rich Silverstein, "On Craft: Writing, Design, and Giving Direction," 8:54.

172 Jeff Goodby and Rich Silverstein, "On Craft: Writing, Design, and Giving Direction," 8:58.

Case Study: Understanding your audience in the workplace

This idea of listening before acting is something Global Talent Management specialist Wangari Kamau learned early on in her career at The World Bank. Working at an international organization, it is particularly important to listen before speaking or attempting to persuade, as colleagues don't possess the same set of cultural norms. With colleagues from South America to Asia to Africa, there was no "safe" approach when dealing with a situation. Every conversation required careful consideration of others' cultural backgrounds.

When I spoke with her, Kamau shared how challenging it is to create the organizational cohesion needed to function well with international colleagues. She emphasized how everyone needs to make an effort to understand where others are coming from before diving into things in order to achieve success. "One thing I believe is listening actively to people, and always approaching things from the perspective of empathy is a great skill," Kamau said. "I know we always hear, but we all have two ears and one mouth for a reason."

Kamau's habit of listening is a skill which allowed her to gain a deep understanding of her colleagues and bosses. Through years of observation, Kamau built a comprehensive personal "database" about those she worked with, including their preferences, personalities, and beliefs. This thorough understanding of her professional audience was indispensable when Kamau found herself in a tricky situation.

After about ten years at The World Bank, Kamau was chatting with some colleagues with similar tenures and expertise when she discovered she was being paid a lot less than some of them. Kamau was puzzled but thought HR had made a simple mistake. So, she asked for a salary review only to be told she didn't need to see the numbers because the reasoning behind her designated pay was sound. Undeterred, Kamau insisted that she review the data herself.

It took her three years to get the data, fighting through institutional bureaucracy and a culture of submission where employees felt they should be grateful for even having a job in the organization. When Kamau saw that the numbers didn't add up, she filed an appeal within the organization's justice system. Something that made her even more confused and convinced that this "data" was a cover-up for other reasons why she wasn't receiving equal pay was the intentionally vague rhetoric in her performance report. The language used in her report skirted around the real reason she wasn't being promoted and paid as her experience and work merited; her efforts were not being equally compensated because she's a Black woman. Reading the thinly veiled sexist and racist language hurt, but it didn't deter Kamau from arguing her case before the internal review court.

Having spent many years listening to and observing her colleagues, superiors, and her general work environment, Kamau was well-positioned to frame and present her case in a way that was most likely to appeal to the board. If Kamau had not acquired a thorough understanding of those around her by listening first, she would have been less aware of what her hostile audience preferred in an argument. This, in turn, would have substantially decreased her chances of succeeding in her appeal.

Based on her past observations, Kamau knew that the review board was resistant to claims of racial discrimination. Accordingly, she avoided framing her petition on that basis. However, Kamau knew that The World Bank was less tolerant of gender discrimination. So, Kamau fought on the grounds of equal pay for equal work over citing the racial undertones of her performance report, which she knew wouldn't be well-received. Equal pay for equal work was an issue the organization was more open to and couldn't ignore. In the end, Kamau won her appeal.

Even though subsequent re-investigations of her salary review granted by the court were hindered by bureaucratic red tape, without a thorough understanding of her audience, Kamau likely wouldn't have won a re-investigation at all. Because she knew her audience well, Kamau didn't back down until she received access to salary data which was a key component she knew the data-obsessed review board would insist on. Rather than risk being caught unprepared and dismissed yet again, Kamau made sure she came into court armed with the documents she needed to make the most persuasive case possible to bosses who relied on data and charts for a living. "You also have to know that when you present things, especially in professional environments, it's very important to have data," Kamau said.

When it comes to standing up for oneself, particularly regarding diversity and inclusion challenges, listening is a key to success. But almost equally important is courage.

"Sometimes you may have a happy ending and sometimes you may not, but for me, the most important thing is for you to stand up and stand in your truth," Kamau said.

Corporate rhetoric

Now that we've seen how listening is a valuable rhetorical tool individuals can use to achieve success in organizations, let's take a look at corporate rhetoric more generally.

How does an organization communicate internally and externally? It's easier to see how an individual giving a speech or writing a book can have a general idea of who their audience is, but for organizations, it's more complex. Imagine you're giving a speech at a TED conference. While the thousands of audience members may come from various backgrounds and lines of work, you can probably expect that they share a mutual love for new information and are curious learners.

However, unlike a speech giver at an academic conference or other events that have a clear target audience, organizations often have to craft rhetorical messages that they want a very broad audience to absorb. This includes customers, but also stakeholders and board members who want to see different, sometimes opposing, company claims. For example, investors will likely feel more comforted by a 50 percent price increase than a 50 percent discount that a customer might enjoy.

George Cheney is a professor of communication at the University of Colorado at Colorado Springs. Cheney conducted an in-depth review of corporate rhetoric and cites a few key aspects that are important to note.[173] First, those inside and outside of a company both see the same corporate rhetoric and come to their own conclusions about how truthful and genuine it is. In order for an organization to be effective, the communications team needs to be able to convey the company's goals and values in a way that resonates with as many people as possible and comes across as sincere. For instance, it would be unwise for a company with a completely white male leadership team to have a prominent banner on its website emphasizing a commitment to "diversity and inclusion." To internal and external observers alike, this would likely come across as disingenuous.

Using rhetoric to build credibility is crucial to gaining people's trust in a company's products and services. As Jude Cohen mentioned in our discussion on advertising, it's increasingly important to consumers that companies "walk the talk." Cheney agrees, and emphasizes how this helps companies build useful credibility. "Consistency and univocality in corporate communication not only facilitate the creation of a distinct identity but also help an organization build credibility among its various audiences," Cheney wrote. "Once established, this credibility becomes a resource for additional communication campaigns...securing maximum impact in a crowded marketplace."

So, not only does putting their wallet where their mouth is build corporate credibility, it helps tie in the various goals and aspects of a company into one cohesive image consumers

173   George Cheney, et. al, "Corporate Rhetoric as Organizational Discourse," *The Sage Handbook of Organizational Discourse*, (London: SAGE Publications Ltd, 2004), 79-104.

can understand and learn to trust. This is particularly useful for large companies that have various functions, products, and services. If you seem like a jack of all trades, without communicating who you are and what you stand for in a simple way consumers can understand, they might not trust you. Worse yet, this might lead them to choose a competitor instead.

Let's bring this to the individual level. Has anyone ever told you that your resume should demonstrate consistency and a clear image of what your career goal is? As someone who has a diverse array of interests, I know my resume often confuses people before I communicate to them how it all ties together. Imagine I tell you my goal is to be a lawyer. You might expect me to be a philosophy or English major, be on Moot Court, Mock Trial, and maybe interning at a law firm. But, if my resume contains other seemingly unrelated pursuits, such as a Biology major, journalism, and some experience in marketing, you might get confused and doubt what my intentions really are.

But, if I constantly emphasize in my cover letter and interview responses how I want to pursue a career in law and how each of these seemingly random pursuits have helped me in my journey, a reassuring credibility and consistency about my career goals can be established.

This all goes to show the important role corporate rhetoric plays in explicitly demonstrating how a company's various pursuits work together to support a handful of professed goals. Organizations, like individuals, are responsible for conveying who they are and what they stand for.

Smart and successful companies often spend a lot of effort trying to get a sense of where the market is heading, how consumers' tastes are changing, and any other applicable trends that will affect their business. They do this through listening to what people are buzzing about and observing what their competitors are doing (i.e., understanding their audience).

Once companies are alerted of a potential change in the environment, say an increasing desire for "clean" personal care products made with minimal ingredients, a company might use rhetoric to communicate how their products have always been organic and vegan (with consistency and credibility helping get this message across). If companies anticipate change, they need to use skilled rhetoric to convey to consumers that they are not only aware of their changing tastes, but have (or will) addressed them. According to Cheney, anticipatory rhetoric helps companies "identify shifting ethical standards, and align company policy and corporate image management accordingly."

While it's great to anticipate changes, what if companies could use rhetoric to shape change? Doing so gives companies a lot more control than just responding to the whims of others. Organizations seeking to differentiate themselves as trend setters rather than simply followers of impending trends can harness rhetoric to influence the public.

Imagine you're a snack company convinced that the future of chips will include healthier options made from superfoods that are packed with vitamins, low-sodium, and low-fat. Picture how powerful it would be if you used rhetoric to convince consumers of the benefits of all of these new features *before* you even launch your product. Through strategic ads and marketing, you could drum up consumer demand that is just dying to try your new chips once they finally hit the market. This is a common strategy social media influencers employ to get faithful followers excited to buy a product created in collaboration with an established company.

While these strategies are powerful if used properly, as we've seen, rhetoric can go both ways. While a master rhetorician is keenly aware and in control of their rhetoric and able to wield it with complete knowledge of its effects, most of us have not reached mastery and are susceptible to our own tools.

If you and your friend both read this book and proceeded to test out strategies on each other, you'd likely still be influenced by quite a few tools, even though you know they're being used against you. Likewise, an organization needs to be aware of how their rhetoric is impacting, and perhaps misleading, organizational leaders themselves. "Not only are organizations often unsuccessful in their attempts to persuade, they may also be unaware of the ultimate effects of their rhetoric," Cheney wrote.

Cheney references the asbestos industry as an example of how being unaware of organizational rhetoric targeted at one's consumers can lead to the organization's own demise. "In its efforts to convince the public of the safety of its product, it ultimately convinced itself that asbestos was safe, leaving it incapable of adequately responding to the chaotic environment faced by the industry once the harmful effects of asbestos were widely recognized," Cheney wrote.

Now, let's discuss how to use rhetoric in a worst-case scenario. When companies are accused of violating ethical codes, social norms, or being offensive to certain groups, they're forced to use "responsive" rhetoric. In a tight spot, companies can always turn to rhetoric to clear the air, perhaps crafting a public statement that communicates why they did (or did not) do something.

Here, once again, listening to and acknowledging your audience is important. It also helps to weave in some humility. "Organizations aim to persuade the public that the crisis is either not their fault or that the organization can resolve the urgent situation," Cheney wrote.

I think most consumers would prefer organizations who choose to use rhetoric to convey the latter. Oftentimes, people just want to hear an "I'm sorry" or "We made a mistake." So, the next time you're in deep water, make sure your rhetoric reflects true remorse and intentions to make things right. Losing others' trust is not worth the few minutes you save resorting to careless rhetoric in times of crisis. Be clear, be direct, and be sincere.

In order to be effective in organizations as an individual, leader, and to be a successful company as a whole, understanding your audience is key. In order to understand your audience, you have to be observant of people's personalities and tendencies, so that when trouble arises you know how to best approach the situation. Whether it's fighting to get your due, providing personal feedback, or trying to make amends with the public, a strategic rhetorical approach can help carry you over the finish line.

Chapter 13

How to Get What You Want

―――

Rhetoric + Everyday Negotiation

Do you ever think of something you really want, then sigh in despair because you're not sure how you're going to get it? Perhaps it's a competitive job, a new computer for Christmas, or finally being able to convince your spouse that a fifty-fifty split on cooking responsibilities is only fair. Whatever your goals may be, everyone has something they want. So, the question I want to explore in this chapter is not "*what* do you want" but "*how* do you get what you want?"

As we've seen, rhetoric is a powerful tool you can use to achieve your goals in various fields and aspects of life. While most of our day-to-day goals are not as ambitious as creating a better pre-med curriculum or winning an election, that doesn't mean our smaller goals are less important.

Imagine you're trying to convince your mom to start getting regular check-ups now that she's "officially" middle aged. But she constantly refuses and attempts to wiggle out of mammograms and other essential health checks by saying "I'll go next year" or "I feel fine." You're at your wits end, simultaneously worried and frustrated. What should you do?

If you're thinking "understand the audience," you're correct. While in this case, you hopefully won't have to spend too much time or effort (she is your mom, after all!), in many situations you may need to do some light background research on the person, organization, or group you're trying to convince to get a better feel for their aspirations, personality, and fears. The important thing to keep in mind is that in order to convince them to act in your favor, you have to understand where they're coming from.

Let's say that it took you two minutes to list out your mom's major personality traits and tendencies. You're all set from the "understanding the audience" front. What do you do next? Step two is to play to your mom's "ego."

Chris St. Hilaire is an award-winning consultant with over twenty years of experience developing communication strategies. His book *27 Powers of Persuasion* mentions several everyday negotiation tips that can help us achieve our goals. The idea behind appealing to someone's "ego" is to play up certain aspects of individuals' sense of self to better convince them to give you what you want.[174]

---

174 Chris St Hilaire and Lynette Padwa, *27 Powers of Persuasion: Simple Strategies to Seduce Audiences & Win Allies* (New York: Prentice Hall Press, 2011).

So, if you know that your mom's worst fear is sitting in a hospital bed, frail and immobile from medical procedures, mentioning that getting regular check-ups can prevent such a situation from happening can help nudge her in the right direction. Or you could play up to her pride in being a responsible mother. You can appeal to this part of her ego by saying something like: "Mom, I've always admired you for being so responsible and proactive. I know that check-ups feel invasive and annoying, but I'm confident that you'll decide to go since you always do the responsible thing."

Another easy tip is to use rhetoric that signals to your opponent that you care about what they think. As Disney CEO Bob Iger mentioned, signaling respect is an important part of communication. Even if you fundamentally disagree with what your opponent thinks, you can still convey respect rhetorically, while incorporating your reality and requests into the conversation. The key here is to "create a common benefit that is your goal."

Now, let's imagine you're facing off with your teenage son who is furious you won't get him AirPods. What should you do? First, resist the urge to hurl back something along the lines of, "Well Jordan, 'just because everyone has them' isn't a good enough reason." Instead, take two seconds to take a deep breath and reach back into your rhetorical toolkit. After taking a moment to recollect everything you've learned about rhetoric, you might say something more conducive to negotiation, such as:

"I get where you're coming from, and your desire to fit in with your friends is totally valid. But, I just spent a lot of money buying you those really nice Patagonia quarter zips for Christmas, so I'd appreciate you understanding that you can't have AirPods right now."

Instead of spitting out a quick rebuttal that lacks respect and empathy, this phrase shows you're recognizing and validating Jordan's perspective. His reality is that he desperately wants to fit in and thinks having AirPods is essential to achieving his goal. However, notice how the response doesn't just validate Jordan's demands but weaves in your request and reality as well. It also leaves open the possibility that Jordan might get AirPods in the future; you're not completely shutting down the idea, but not giving in either.

Sometimes, we know that our audience's ego won't allow them to just accept our idea. In this situation, you can try to use your understanding of her/him to get them to come up with the suggestion *you* have in mind, giving off the illusion that they came up with this idea independently. Because everything you say is inevitably filtered through your audience's experiences, it can be hard to control how they view your request. So if you're tasked with negotiating with a hostile audience member, it's smart to avoid arguing that your way is better. Instead, focus on nudging them into suggesting your request themselves.

Let's say your partner is a terrible cook. Because you love and admire them, the last thing you want to do is say "Hey, I love you and all, but you really need to take some cooking lessons." A conversation with this opener would go particularly poorly if you have a partner who has a huge ego, or is just really insecure about their cooking skills already. With that route crossed off the map, you can employ this idea of rhetorical nudging to get your partner to suggest cooking lessons him/herself. It could go something like this:

"I'm sorry that you feel like the roast chicken was a failure, Wil. I know you put a lot of time and effort into it. Do you think there's anyone who could help you figure out what went wrong?"

Now, note that you're not introducing the idea that the roast chicken was a failure. If you did that, you might as well abandon any attempts to be rhetorically savvy. But most people know when something is a catastrophe. Once they've had the self-awareness to offhandedly mention the obvious, you can seize the opportunity to steer their thought-process towards a favorable solution for you. Remember to watch your tone, keeping it neutral and not blameful, while suggesting that there's a way Wil can feel better about himself and the roast chicken.

After your nudge, Wil might bring up himself that he could probably use a teacher to help him learn how to cook better. Then, you could offer to look up some great cooking classes in the area and you're on your way to achieving your goal of helping Wil and your appetite.

Case Study: High-stakes negotiation skills

Let's build off of St. Hilaire's tips with a few from Chris Voss. Voss was the lead international kidnapping negotiator for the Federal Bureau of Investigation (FBI), serving as the FBI's hostage negotiation representative for the National Security

Council's Hostage Working Group. After working for twenty-four years at the FBI, in 2008 Voss left to found the Black Swan Group, teaching business professionals to better their outcomes by using the same negotiating tools he depended upon to save lives. He's also the author of a book on negotiation titled *Never Split the Difference: Negotiating As If Your Life Depended On It*.[175]

In addition to his training by the FBI, Voss was trained in negotiation by the London Police force Scotland Yard and at Harvard Law school. Perhaps Voss' cross-industry rhetorical training isn't so surprising, now that we've learned that mastering the art of rhetoric requires you to cross seemingly firm industry borders. Voss is an expert in teaching others the rhetorical tools he's perfected over the years, often in high-stakes life or death situations. The majority of his tips include using subtle, strategic rhetoric tools to influence your opponent without them even realizing that you're guiding their thinking.

When you're at the negotiating table, you're typically already seen as the antagonist by your opponent. Usually, both sides are gathering to find common ground that neither side really wants to concede. In order to open up the conversation and encourage opponents to talk, Voss recommends using the idea of "mirroring." Mirroring entails choosing one to three words from your opponent's most recent response (or the conversation more generally) to incorporate into the beginning of your response.

---

175 Christopher Voss and Tahl Raz, *Never Split the Difference: Negotiating as If Your Life Depended on It* (London: RH Business Books, 2016).

Imagine you're in a heated mergers and acquisition (M&A) talk and your opponent Sylvia shoots back with "The price is too high." You think she's bluffing, but you're not 100 percent sure. You can use mirroring to move the conversation forward simply by repeating, "The price is too high?" Mirroring what your opponent says makes them feel listened to which prompts them to further elaborate on their statement. This allows you to coax out your opponent's true sources of objection without you having to give away your thoughts on their response or offer. "They're going to go on and elaborate, and they're going to give me context," Voss said. "They're going to feel like I'm working with them. They're not going to feel me fighting."[176]

In contrast, directly asking "Why is the price too high?" may trigger a more defensive response, encouraging Sylvia to close off or double down on her insistence that the price needs to be lower.

While mirroring is an incredibly powerful rhetorical tool that helps build trust and curiosity at the outset, combined with another tool called "labeling," it's even more effective. "Labeling" enables you to get even more information out of your opponent, all without you having to offer any information back in return. Voss calls labeling the most useful tool in business, and once again, it's almost deceivingly simple. You can use labels to verbally express your observations of how the other person is feeling. While it may be easy in some situations to offer a label that is accurate, it doesn't necessarily matter if you hit the nail on the head.

---

176 Chris Voss, "Mirroring," in Chris Voss Teaches The Art of Negotiation, November 13, 2020, MasterClass video, 6:54.

In order to respond to your label, your opponent has to take a moment to self-reflect on how they are feeling. This prompted extra beat or two in between a heated exchange can be particularly helpful when your opponent is experiencing a negative emotion like anger and could use a few seconds to calm down. This strategy can help protect whoever is at risk in the conversation by slowing down the pacing of the exchange.

Let's continue our negotiation with Sylvia. Let's say that after you mirror her, she responds with "Yeah, the price is too high. How do you think the board is going to feel about me trading away so many of our assets to acquire your company? You're making this potential partnership cost more than it's worth." While you may be tempted to defend your company's value, resist the urge to fight back. Instead, use a label. You might say something like, "It sounds like you're upset about the price" or "It seems like you're under a lot of pressure to deliver a good deal to the board."

With these labels, Sylvia will be further encouraged to elaborate on whether she really feels "X" way or not, and if so, why. Using mirroring and labeling to gain extra background information on your opponent's situation, particularly when it's unclear, will help you rhetorically frame your response in a more advantageous way. The best part is that you can "recycle" these strategies, employing labeling and mirroring multiple times throughout a conversation to follow up on any new information your opponent has just revealed.

In fact, research has shown that labeling "can attenuate our emotional experiences." UCLA researchers Jared Toore and Matthew Liberman call *affect labeling* "putting feelings into words." Affect labeling is essentially what Voss is suggesting we all do. Toore and Liberman have found that while affect labeling does not "feel like a regulatory process as it occurs," it "produces a pattern of effects like those seen during explicit emotion regulation."[177]

In other words, affect labeling is a form of implicit emotional regulation which is considered "automatic;" this means that it happens unconsciously.[178] Because it happens unconsciously, affect labeling influences us without us even being aware of it. Nudging people in ways they don't anticipate, or mentally process, gives you the upper hand. You know these techniques draw out valuable information, but your opponent is blissfully unaware. As a result, they will unconsciously keep talking and talking, giving away valuable information on their situation and true motivations, leaving them vulnerable in a negotiation.

But it's still important to be careful of your rhetoric when you label. Notice how Voss recommends using statements that put the focus on your opponent and how they're feeling (or how you think they're feeling), instead of what you think. Using a phrase like "What I'm hearing is..." is an example of labeling you should avoid. "By starting out with 'what I'm hearing is,' I've dropped the word 'I' in inappropriately and the message I'm conveying is that I'm more interested in my perspective than yours," Voss said.[179]

177 Jared B. Torre, and Matthew D. Lieberman, "Putting Feelings Into Words: Affect Labeling as Implicit Emotion Regulation," *Emotion Review* 10, no. 2 (April 2018): 116–24.

178 A. Gyurak., J. J. Gross, & A. Etkin, "Explicit and implicit emotion regulation: a dual-process framework," *Cognition & emotion* 25, no. 3 (2011): 400–412.

179 Chris Voss, "Labeling," 4:22.

It seems like a really small nit-picky thing, but that's part of the art of mastering rhetoric—every word counts and has an impact on the listener. Simply replacing "you" with "I" changes the whole connotation of your observation and can cause your attempt at labeling to backfire.

While we've explored how labels can be used to define a negative emotion, you can also use it to validate your opponents' emotions. This can make your opponent feel like you understand where they're coming from which makes them more willing to hear you out. Here's a practical example of when you can use labeling to emphasize a positive trait to your advantage.

Imagine you're faced with a customer service representative who sounds cranky and isn't being the most sympathetic to your requests. It may be tempting to retaliate in a similar tone, but Voss encourages people to keep their cool and use this opportunity to try their hand at improving their fortunes through labeling.

To label, you'll have to think of the situation from the customer service representative's perspective, who we'll call Lulu. Lulu has probably been on the phone with angry, rude customers for hours and is feeling pretty irritated and disrespected. She might be nearing the end of her workday and anxious to get back home, pick her kids up from childcare, and unwind a bit before repeating everything the next day. Imagine if you said: "I feel like you're being very generous with your time right now and are tired of dealing with customers like me."

Lulu will probably be a bit surprised, but agree that she is indeed very tired of addressing entitled customers' needs.

By labeling the situation in a way you can anticipate and that paints Lulu in a positive light, you're signaling that you understand her situation. This signal of empathy and understanding will likely trigger reciprocal feelings in Lulu who may work harder to address your concerns than if you had simply stated them, like every other customer.

A similar rhetorical technique is something Voss calls "the accusations audit." This is when you mentally take stock of the worst things your opponent could be thinking about you. Don't shy away from including extreme conclusions, like, "Wow, Rachel is an annoying imbecile who doesn't know what she's talking about." It may hurt a bit, but to be a skilled negotiator you need to consider everything your opponent could throw at you, whether it's reasonable or not. Once you have a brief list of the worst-case scenarios, you can address these potential elephants in the room before they burst onto the scene. "Unexpressed negative emotions never die," Voss said "They become cancerous. This is an approach to go after these and even get in front of them and trigger a working collaborative relationship from the very beginning."[180]

Let's return once more to our example with Sylvia who we're still negotiating a deal with. You can tell she's upset and defensive and generally unhappy in her current situation. You can say something like:

"I know I seem like I'm a know-it-all and the last person on earth you'd want to be talking to right now. You probably think I'm an incompetent jerk who's wasting your time."

---

180 Chris Voss, "The Accusations Audit," 1:56.

While it may be uncomfortable to suggest such things about yourself, this technique helps trigger empathy and prompts your opponent to say "no" instead of "yes." Saying no feels noncommittal, and this technique helps guide your opponent to reconsider their assumptions about you and/or the situation without feeling like they're being pushed to do so. It gives your opponent the illusion of control and the upper hand even though with mirroring, labeling, and the accusations audit, you're guiding them away from their hardline stance.

Using an accusations audit to build up a worst-case scenario and then suggest an idea that, by comparison doesn't seem that bad at all, can be another spin on this technique. Voss describes how he uses juxtaposition in accusations audits to get late hotel check outs all the time. Here's how it goes: Instead of begging the hotel clerk to let you check out late, you could introduce the subject with: "I'm going to sound like the most horrible guest ever." And then, you can insert your request to have a late check out which is probably far from the worst-case scenario the hotel clerk was thinking of (or has experienced).

This introduction creates an automatic sense of grateful relief in your opponent which makes them much more likely to grant your request. The hotel clerk could've been expecting you to describe how you threw an impromptu party in your hotel room last night and how all of the furniture is destroyed and covered with vomit. So, they will likely be pleased that you're "only" asking for a late checkout.

Let's revisit the idea of mirroring for a second. While we can mirror our opponent's words, we can also encourage our opponent to mirror our tone. This time, you're taking the lead and getting the other party to respond at your pace. Research has shown that "mirror neurons" do exist which sheds light on why these mirroring techniques work so well.

In their study, researchers Sourya Acharya and Samarth Shukla explored how mirror neurons "respond to actions that we observe in others." The way mirror neurons work is that they "fire in the same way when we actually recreate that action ourselves." That's powerful because that means mirror neurons make our brains think we're actually experiencing the same situation someone else is presenting, when we're not.[181]

We won't get into the neuroscience details, but Voss uses this idea of mirror neurons to guide opponents' thinking with the tone of his voice, particularly in tense situations. To calm people down, he'll use his slow "radio host" voice. To avoid outright arguments, he tries to keep his voice neutral and avoid sounding too assertive. Because of mirror neurons, when Voss' opponent hears how calm he is, they'll unconsciously slow down and become calmer too. Much of this relates to lawyer Hemma Lomax's comment on tone and body language as well. Everything sends a message and can add to (or detract from) your rhetorical effectiveness, so it's important to use these techniques to your advantage.

Let's wrap it up with one last tip: replace "why" with "what" or "how." The reason behind this switch is that "what" and

---

181 S. Acharya, & S. Shukla, "Mirror neurons: Enigma of the metaphysical modular brain," *Journal of natural science, biology, and medicine* 3, no. 2 (2012): 118–124.

"how" questions tend to encourage further elaboration without the defensiveness. "People love to be asked what to do," Voss said. "People love to be asked how to do something. 'Why' as a question triggers defensiveness, universally. 'Why' makes you feel accused."

For example, if my friend Yamei asks me if I like a sweater that I think looks ridiculous, instead of saying "Why do you like it?" I can ask "So, how do you think you're going to incorporate this into an outfit?"

By using "what" and "how" questions, you can guide your opponent's thinking with probing questions that don't seem to attack their judgement. And, once I ask enough how and what questions, such as "What will you do with it if you end up not liking it?" I can nudge Yamei closer and closer to deciding not to buy the sweater. Even if I successfully convince Yamei to abandon the sweater through my questioning, she will probably feel like she came to that conclusion on her own. And, that type of unconscious persuasion is what is needed in many delicate situations.

A lot of these tips may sound extremely manipulative, and in a way, they are. But the reason we're learning rhetorical techniques is to use them for good. Voss used these techniques to save lives, getting staunch political or religious opponents to give up hostages. Now, he's using them to get businesses to be more effective in achieving their goals. So, now that you're aware of these tools, I encourage you to use them in your professional and personal life, but within reason and with good cause.

Adjusting your persuasive strategy

Now that we've learned about specific negotiation techniques we can use in our everyday lives, it's important to zoom back out and think about what general negotiation category a specific situation falls into. Knowing not only your goal, but the context of what you're asking for can be useful in shaping your argumentation in an appropriate manner. Taking the time to reflect on the situational aspects of your request can also help you prepare better responses for the many rejections that may come your way.

In a recent *Harvard Business Review* article, Hannah Bowles, who we met earlier in the chapter on business, highlighted three main types of negotiation: asking, bending, and shaping. Asking negotiations adhere neatly to the status quo; the request is usually something pretty standard for a professional in a certain role or with a certain amount of experience. Bending negotiations are a bit trickier, as they entail asking for special treatment that goes against the current company norms. Shaping negotiations can shake up an entire industry and include bold proposals to completely change the organizational environment you're in. "Depending on whether you are in an asking, a bending, or a shaping negotiation, you will need to vary your arguments to win your counterparts' support," Bowles wrote.[182]

While asking negotiations can involve a simple quid pro quo structure if you're asked to perform an additional

---

182 Hannah Riley Bowles and Bobbi Thomason, "Negotiating Your Next Job," *Harvard Business Review*, December 15, 2020.

role that is outside of your domain in exchange for your request, bending negotiations require extensive pre-negotiation preparation. Bowles recommends listing out every potential reason why your boss would support your request and then coming up with a list of possible reasons why they might still reject your proposal. Then, Bowles suggests going through each point and coming up with a counterargument. It's smart to be prepared, particularly when heading into a risky negotiation that can affect your image within a company.

In Bowles' research, shaping negotiations were often used by executive women who chose to forge their own path. "One of the real insights that came out of that work was how much these women were really changing their working environments through the negotiation,'" Bowles said. "[Negotiation] is a way of using words to change the world...whether that's around work and family, or whether that's about advancing women into positions for which they do not have the typical qualifications."

Because they were armed with research about what is negotiable, reasons why their proposals could be rejected, and to what extent their proposal is bending the "way things are," these women were rhetorically prepared to change not only companies, but entire industries. With a strong hold on rhetoric in negotiation, these female executives were able to create new paths for not only themselves but those after them.

How you say it matters

People flooded the streets of New York City, decked out in their masks and honking their horns in celebration of Joe Biden's presidential election victory. Elsewhere in the country, people protested, outraged and unmasked. In today's increasingly complex, and often divided world, it's easy to pigeonhole yourself into a certain set of ideas or beliefs. Pew Research recently conducted a survey that showed 64 percent of Republicans see Democrats as more close-minded than the average American, and 75 percent of Democrats think the same for Republicans. As attacks and mistrust have turned increasingly personal, it's perhaps not surprising that people in opposite parties often view each other not only as wrong, but immoral. Fifty-five percent of Republicans hold this view about Democrats, while 46 percent of Democrats feel the same about Republicans.[183]

With an increasingly polarized political climate, the US has become an unfortunate example of how easy it is for citizens to close themselves off from diversity of thought. But, while we may never learn to love our enemies, rhetoric is a powerful tool we can use in our daily lives to foster tolerance for and understanding of those different from us.

Imagine if someone came up to you and said something along the lines of "That's such a stupid idea. Why would you ever believe such a thing?" Even if you have thicker skin than most people, such a response would probably still sting

---

183 "Partisan Antipathy: More Intense, More Personal," *Pew Research Center - U.S. Politics & Policy*, August 17, 2020.

a little. But what is it about this response that makes it feel so hurtful?

Sometimes, it's not the fact that you're right or wrong that makes you feel personally attacked. In many situations, the accuracy of someone's comment may not even be in question. What is making you feel agitated and insulted is the *way* someone said something. When broaching a sensitive controversial subject with loved ones, it's easy to brush aside the pleasantries and delve shamelessly into a heated debate. But research shows that it is during such conversations, and sometimes negotiations, where watching one's tone and rhetoric is key.

University of California researchers Shrikanth Narayanan and Panayiotis Georgiou, alongside M.D. Nasir and collaborator Dr. Brian Baucom of University of Utah, have shown that in an argument with those nearest and dearest, such as your spouse, tone can matter more than the content. "What you say is not the only thing that matters, it's very important how you say it," Nasir said. "Our study confirms that it holds for a couple's relationship as well."

Central to people's ability to address a point of contention in a beneficial manner is the ability to separate yourself from the heated emotions you may be experiencing. While it's important to acknowledge your emotions, in tense situations fueling the fire can make matters worse.

Instead, Narayanan et al. suggest that we take a moment to logically think through how our opponent's rhetoric is making us feel. Instead of giving in to an emotional outburst, during a confrontation we should strive to calmly reflect on negative feelings and how those negative feelings are connected to what our loved one just said about us. "It's not just about studying your emotions," Narayanan said. "It's about studying the impact of what your partner says on your emotions."[184]

This idea of taking a few seconds to survey, digest, and label the emotional landscape is a rhetorical skill that Voss suggested we use to guide others' emotions. But it's also a tool we can use on ourselves.

Conveying an openness to listen and learn

Now that we know one way to respond when we're feeling attacked rhetorically, let's look at some strategies we can use when we're the one making divisive claims. While many of us likely profess that we think it's okay for others to have opinions that are different than ours, oftentimes the way we communicate doesn't convey open-mindedness. But, there are ways we can demonstrate humility and a willingness to learn without backing down from our position on an issue.

When we're discussing an issue we have strong opinions on, it's easy to snap at your opponent because you care deeply about the subject. Typically, we care about what we believe in, so it's natural to feel defensive when others question our core beliefs. Sometimes, these beliefs guide our life philosophy,

---

184 Matthew P. Black et al., "Toward Automating a Human Behavioral Coding System for Married Couples' Interactions Using Speech Acoustic Features," *Speech Communication* 55, no. 1, (2013): 1-21.

which makes it even harder to be willing to listen to others challenge them. But, demonstrating a willingness to listen is essential in having conversations that will enable us to build a bridge of understanding, if not agreement, with others on important issues. This is particularly critical when attempting to negotiate with others on.

Keith Stanovich of the University of Toronto and Richard F. West of James Madison University distinguish thought into "system 1" or "system 2" ways of thinking. Those who employ "system 1" rely heavily on intuition, which is a fast response often described as automatic and highly emotional. In contrast, "system 2" is much slower because it tries to be logical. Thus, careful thinking often involves "system 2" thought, while speedy decisions rely on "system 1" thought.[185]

In heated conversations, about politics or religion for example, it's easy to default to our "system 1" way of thinking; it's easier, quicker, and allows us to indulge in emotional highs and lows. Sometimes, this means that we're so absorbed in our train of thought that we neglect to listen. We forget to listen in order to understand potential sources of our opponent's bias. This is a loss of valuable information because, as we've learned, understanding where others are coming from is often necessary in order to move the conversation forward.

Princeton University psychologist Daniel Kahneman and Australian Graduate School of Management psychologist Daniel Lovallo argue that we often make decisions using

---

185   PON Staff, "Essential Negotiation Skills: Limiting Cognitive Bias in Negotiation: Essential Business Negotiation Strategies and Tactics to Create Value at the Bargaining Table," Harvard Law School, January 21, 2021.

either an "insider lens" or "outsider lens." When we're "deeply immersed in a particular context or situation," we often rely on "system 1 thought" and make decisions that are intuitive and emotional. But, what we want to do is slow down, using "system 2" thought and an outsider lens. This allows us to take stock of how someone outside our group might believe something different than us.

However, a prerequisite of employing the outsider lens and "system 2" thought is to detach ourselves from the emotions of a situation. While tricky to do in the moment, it's more strategic to use an "outsider lens" when trying to spur dialogue in a productive direction.[186]

We've covered a lot of ground in this chapter on how to negotiate everyday matters, in addition to those that are higher stakes. With so many different rhetorical tools available to us, it can be easy to forget how to use them. That's why these tools need to not only be understood theoretically, but refined through practice. This is the key to successfully and effortlessly incorporating these strategies into your everyday life. Getting started can be intimidating, but it's important to begin practicing during less consequential negotiations. That way, when a more important matter comes up, you can confidently outmaneuver your opponent.

---

186 Ibid.

Chapter 14

Careful What You Say

——

Rhetoric + Mental Health

Imagine you're catching up with one of your best friends at dinner, and then he turns to you and says, "I've been struggling with anxiety and depression for fifteen years now." You're shocked, but you don't want to give off the impression that you believe having a mental illness is something they should be wary of sharing. So, perhaps you decide to just nod, thank him for sharing, and move the conversation along. Or you might begin to panic a bit because you're not sure how to show your friend that you care for and value them regardless of any mental health struggles. You might be sitting there sweating through the seat of your pants, wondering desperately, *What do I say?*

Chances are, you've had a similar experience to the one described above. According to the National Institutes of Mental Health, one in five US adults has a mental illness, which in 2017 totaled to 46.6 million people.[187] With the prevalence of mental illness, you might be wondering why we still find it so hard to talk about it with friends and loved ones. If you've had an experience where you were at a loss for words, not sure how to navigate a conversation surrounding mental health, you're not alone. It can be difficult, even for medical professionals, to know the right rhetoric to use when talking through mental health challenges with others.

While there is not a one size fits all rhetorical solution to discussing something as personal as mental health challenges, there are simple ways we can all adjust our rhetoric to better support those in our lives who struggle with mental illnesses. One important aspect of support is being able to effectively convey our empathy and a willingness to listen.

While most people approach sensitive topics with good intentions, using common, seemingly comforting phrases such as "I understand" can actually be a turn-off. In a mental health awareness training I completed at Vanderbilt University, therapists and clinical psychiatrists emphasized the power of adjusting that phrase to "I want to understand."[188]

When you were a teenager, did your dad ever say, "I understand where you're coming from" in a way that only made you more upset and angrier? Imagine you're a Gen Z teen and you have a friend named David who is bent on getting an Apple Watch. One day, you're at his house and witness an outburst. Angered by a well-meaning "I understand" form

187 "Mental Illness," *National Institute of Mental Health*, U.S. Department of Health and Human Services, January 2021.
188 "Center for Student Wellbeing," Vanderbilt University.

his dad, David exclaims, "Of course you wouldn't understand, Dad. You're ancient and don't even know how to power off your phone!"

Although the accusation of being "ancient" is an exaggeration, there is a kernel of truth in the above response. If David's dad was born in the 60s and grew up in the 80s when Apple was still a start-up, he probably can't really relate to his need to have the latest tech devices. To him, any current technology might still be a marvel, causing him to view requests for the most cutting-edge devices as unnecessary. So, when David's dad professes that he "understands" David's situation, which is impacted by the tech-heavy world he grew up in, it's easier to see why this phrase could rub him the wrong way.

Oftentimes, statements such as "I understand" are offered with the intention of comforting someone else. But, when there is no way you can actually understand a person's situation, using this phrase can make matters worse. Rather than demonstrating empathy and an open ear, you're suggesting that you already know the details of their struggles. The frustration and annoyance that David felt is something that we can spare those battling mental illnesses. Just like how David's dad couldn't truly understand how having an Apple Watch could make his tech-filled lifestyle even better, insisting that you "understand" what it's like to have depression (or another mental illness) when you don't can be infuriating and hurtful.

Most of us have probably professed to "understand" something we couldn't possibly relate to when speaking with others. Maybe it was insisting that you totally get how difficult your friend's engineering coursework is even though you've never taken a college-level STEM class, or that you understand how hard it is to lose a parent even though you've never experienced that loss. Instead of moving the conversation forward with false statements of understanding that make us feel more caring and at ease, but hurt those we're trying to comfort, we should focus on shifting our rhetoric. A simple change to "I *want* to understand" or "I'm *trying* to understand" can make all the difference.

Let's revisit our scenario with David. Imagine if his dad said something along the lines of, "I want to understand why getting an Apple Watch is so important to you. To me, it seems like a duplicate of an iPhone, which you already have. I'm willing to change my mind, but I'll need some help understanding where you're coming from."

While David's dad is not necessarily conceding to David's outburst or changing his stance, he is framing his response in a way that acknowledges that he *doesn't* quite get why David is making such a fuss. Because it rhetorically demonstrates that he has an open ear, this response encourages David to open up further. If David's dad wanted to take his response to the next level, he might also throw in some labeling, an "accusations audit," and use "how" instead of "why" to get a better negotiation going:

"It feels like you're really upset, and that you're going to think I'm the absolute worst dad in the whole world if I don't buy you an Apple Watch. How is an Apple watch going to better fulfill your current needs?"

While claiming an understanding of someone's situation can cause them to clam up, since you are suggesting you don't need any further explanation, clearly stating that you don't understand but want to can be a powerful tool. And it doesn't hurt to throw in some of those tried and true negotiation techniques to encourage David to further elaborate on his inner motivations without seeming like you're pushing him too hard.

A similar rhetorical adjustment can and should be used to better support those struggling with mental illnesses. Mental illnesses are still commonly stigmatized, so for therapists, health professionals, and everyday people to achieve our goal of better supporting those who are facing these illnesses, it's imperative that we make slight shifts in our everyday rhetoric to show we're open to learning and listening.[189]

In addition to the simple shift from saying "I understand" to "I want to understand," there are other rhetorical techniques we can use to show others that we're open-minded, ready to listen, and support them in their personal challenges. Mental Health First Aid (MHFA) provides everyday citizens with training on how to "identify, understand, and respond to signs of mental illness and substance disorders." Having trained over 2.5 million Americans, MHFA has a few easy rhetorical tips we can use to help those around us.[190]

Step one is to be a good listener. In a conversation with a loved one about mental health, our goal is to persuade them

189 P. W. Corrigan, & A. C. Watson, "Understanding the impact of stigma on people with mental illness," *World Psychiatry* 1, no. 1 (2002): 16–20.
190 "About MHFA," *Mental Health First Aid*, February 16, 2021.

to take steps to take better care of themselves and perhaps seek professional help. So, showing that you're an active listener by making eye contact, nodding as appropriate, and refraining from making judgmental faces is one critical aspect of being an effective rhetorician in this situation. You might even lean forward in your chair when someone is opening up to you, like Robin Roberts does, to physically demonstrate your interest and care.[191]

Something to avoid is jumping straight into offering "solutions" to your friend's struggles. Sometimes, as listeners not involved in the particular situation, we are so busy thinking about ways we can help that we're not giving others the space to get everything off of their chest and vent a little. There'll be time later to discuss next steps, so in the moment, focus your energies on demonstrating strong listening skills and not jumping to assuming what others need.

Related to our discussion above, is step two: don't make assumptions.[192] As tempting as it is to think something like "Well, calculus can't be that bad" or "losing your job isn't the end of the world," offering your well-intentioned diagnosis or suggestions can do more harm than good. When we start to think that others are judging us, or not paying attention, it's easy to shut down and give up on explaining yourself further. It is especially important to avoid this when a friend is opening up to you because they need help.

---

191 Mental Health First Aid USA, "The Quiet Power of Empathic Listening," *Mental Health First Aid*, July 28, 2017.

192 "Friendship and Mental Health," *Mental Health Foundation*, August 14, 2018.

Along the same vein, step three is making sure you stick to open-ended questions. It's easy to unintentionally signal our inner thoughts with the words and phrasing we use. When we use close-ended questions or statements like "Does that make you feel down?" we're already inserting our own opinions and thoughts into the conversation. Here, I'm suggesting that whatever happened is making my friend feel sad, when instead, it could be making him feel something entirely different (i.e., joy) or more complex (for example, feeling wistful). While there can be a time and place for close-ended questions further down the line, when someone is unloading something personal and distressing, it's probably not the time to tell them what *you* think. Instead, asking a simple "How does that make you feel?" can keep the conversation focused on your friend and not you. Note how we're choosing to use a "how" question instead of "why do you feel that way." This goes back to Voss' point on avoiding "why" questions that might trigger defensiveness.

Those are just a few tips to start us off, but with mindful awareness and by slowly incorporating those slight rhetorical shifts into our everyday conversations, we can become better friends, listeners, and advocates for those who need us the most. Paying attention to how you convey your care can be incredibly impactful. In fact, it can even help save lives.

Avoiding dehumanizing language in medicine

Have you ever thought to yourself, *Why does medical language have to be so complicated?* Whether it's the twelve plus letter drug names like Dextromethorphan that trip you up or the long names of diseases that always seem to have some researcher's last name in the middle, complex medical rhetoric can be confusing at best. While it can be helpful and necessary to have standardized names for diseases, drugs, and devices to promote efficient conversation, sometimes patients' stories get lost in all that jargon. Instead of being seen as a person with a medical challenge, sticking to medical rhetoric alone can shift the focus to the medical challenge first and person second.[193]

This type of dehumanization can be worsened when medical terms are used unnecessarily as a part of everyday medical rhetoric. In her book *Patient Tales: Case Histories and the Uses of Narrative in Psychiatry*, Carol Berkenkotter laments how "richly descriptive narratives get lost in the rhetorical-linguistic strategies that caregivers are mandated to use to make and lend credence to their diagnoses."[194] Because our stories and experiences are what humanizes us and make us unique, overshadowing important narratives, particularly as they pertain to our medical health, can be a way medical rhetoric is more detrimental than helpful.

How would you feel if you were chatting with a therapist, describing how you think everything is falling apart, and saw that all he wrote down on his notepad is "John has predominantly dysphoric mood"? Or, imagine you confessed that perhaps you were a bit too needy in a relationship that fell apart,

193 Abdullah Awaysheh et al., "A review of medical terminology standards and structured reporting," *Journal of Veterinary Diagnostic Investigation* 30, no. 1 (2018): 17-25.

194 Carol Berkenkotter, *Patient Tales: Case Histories and the Uses of Narrative in Psychiatry* (Columbia: University of South Carolina Press, 2008).

but your psychiatrist simply wrote down "adjustment disorder with depressed mood." I'm guessing that you're not feeling too happy about either of those scenarios; I know I would be offended and a bit hurt if that's all I saw scribbled down after I poured out my heart and soul in an hour long therapy session.

In some situations, sticking to proper rhetoric can alienate and "otherize" those we are trying to help. In the realm of mental health, it's particularly important to avoid such rhetoric that focuses on the challenge at hand more than the person. In fact, rhetoric in the mental health field has such a large impact that it's been seriously studied for years. Let's delve into some suggestions researchers have on how we can avoid stigmatizing rhetoric in our everyday conversations.

One example of a simple rhetorical shift we can all make in our everyday lives to decrease the stigma surrounding mental illness is Arthur Kleinman's distinction between "disease" and "illness."[195] Kleinman is a Professor of Medical Anthropology in Global Health and Social Medicine and Professor of Psychiatry at Harvard University. In his book *The Illness Narratives: Suffering, Healing, And The Human Condition*, Kleinman explores how calling mental health challenges an "illness" rather than a "disease" can encourage medical professionals to acknowledge the human behind the mental health struggle, rather than overfocusing on the medical challenge itself.

While these words may sound one and the same, Kleinman discusses how "disease is concerned with organic origins

---

195 "Arthur Kleinman," Anthropology Department, accessed February 20, 2021.

of pathologies as they are described in medical texts" while "illness" "involves the everyday problems that living patients encounter."

So, if I describe Brianna as struggling with a "disease," I'm suggesting that the entirety of her experiences and challenges can be summed up by her medical diagnosis. On the other hand, if I talk about Brianna's "illness," I'm highlighting how "dynamic" her day-to-day challenges are. This language reminds others that Brianna's struggles weren't resolved upon diagnosis but are an ongoing battle. Adjusting our rhetoric is a way we can guide others towards empathy and acceptance, instead of judgement and dismissal, of patients' challenges.

Cathryn Molloy, an Associate Professor at James Madison University, conducted an intriguing study centered around "recuperative ethos." In other words, Molloy studied the way patients experiencing mental health challenges used rhetoric to re-establish their credibility. Because mental illness still has quite a bit of negative stigma surrounding it, it's not surprising that Molloy found patients who were using language and storytelling to fight against others' assumptions about them.[196]

In her study, Molloy found that "participants threaded indications of their astuteness, their social intelligences and educational achievements, their knowledge of great works and their ability to incisively unpack esoteric content into their everyday conversations."

---

196 Cathryn Molloy, "Recuperative ethos and agile epistemologies: Toward a vernacular engagement with mental illness ontologies," *Rhetoric Society Quarterly* 45, no. 2 (2015): 138-163.

Because patients were used to being seen as "problematic," or "unstable," they felt the need to incorporate experiences and words that demonstrated their ability to establish stable human connections and even verify their educational level in their everyday rhetoric. "Since they have been diagnosed with illnesses that affect the brain and since pharmaceutical interventions are known to cloud thinking, they want to convince listeners of their exceptional intelligence," Molloy wrote.

Not only do medical providers, family, and friends shift their rhetoric when confronting mental illnesses, patients do too. Rhetoric can be an important tool that patients use to redefine themselves in the face of many (sometimes negative) assumptions about them. Rhetoric can help them reclaim the agency denied by their friends, family, strangers, and even healthcare providers.

When medical rhetoric is emphasized at the expense of patients' stories and dehumanization, it's time to think about ways we can shift rhetoric surrounding illness away from relying on strict medical terminology to convey patients' challenges. Being careful of what terms we use to describe people's health matters. Simply swapping out "disease" for "illness" can make all the difference in showing how someone's health challenges extend beyond their diagnosis and continues to impact their day to day lives.

When we continue to have societal stigma around mental illnesses, patients feel the need to redeem themselves and use the power of rhetoric to assert their competence and ability. Mental health is a complex topic that's hard to be completely prepared to discuss. But, with our rhetorical tools in mind, including these new tips more directly related to navigating sensitive subjects with others, we can be more persuasive and helpful to those around us. While this chapter focused on the practical impact rhetoric can have on one everyday challenge, these techniques can be applied to various other situations we encounter to better support those around us.

Chapter 15

Dangers of Rhetoric

We've spent a lot of time exploring how rhetoric is a powerful tool that is applicable to everything in our lives. We've seen how people use rhetorical tools on us, and how we can use them to influence others. We've discussed how key techniques, including understanding your audience, framing, and intentional nonverbal cues, can be applied to fields ranging from politics to science to business. At this point in our journey, I hope you feel well equipped to begin practicing these tools in your everyday life and make them work for you.

I want to round out our discussion on everyday rhetoric by exploring the ways we should *not* use rhetoric. As we've seen, rhetoric is impactful, and can have far reaching effects on others (intended and unintended). Unfortunately, similar to other powerful skills, rhetoric can be used for harm.

While all of us have different spectrums of morality we abide by, I hope we can all agree that rhetoric should not be used to intentionally harm or take advantage of others. Granted, the idea of "harm" in itself is subjective. You could argue that using rhetorical tools to get patients to accept the treatment they need, which may be physically and emotionally painful, and expensive, is using rhetoric for harm. Indeed, the idea of whether to suggest treatment and if so, what type, is a question doctors constantly grapple with. But, on the other hand, some of you may insist that doctors who use rhetoric to convince patients to go through with painful treatments that end up prolonging their life in a meaningful way create a net benefit that outweighs any harm done.

While "harm" is up to interpretation, I'll use the Hippocratic oath of "first, do no harm," combined with a healthy dose of common sense and a (hopefully) standard moral compass, to guide my interpretation of what it means to use rhetoric for harm.[197]

Case study: Medicine

Let's stick with the field of medicine for a moment. Earlier, Dr. Marty Makary revealed how rhetoric is often used to "nudge" patients to accept expensive treatments that are not the best ones available. In his book, Makary explores the darker side of these nudges that, in Dr. Victor Wu's experience, can be extremely helpful when used by honest, well-meaning doctors who deeply care about their patients.

He highlights certain "trigger words" that some doctors use to make their lives easier, and patients' lives harder. "Every

---

197 "Greek Medicine - The Hippocratic Oath," *U.S. National Library of Medicine*, National Institutes of Health, February 7, 2012.

specialty has its phrases," Makary wrote. "For obstetricians, it's saying something like, 'It might be safer for the baby.'"[198]

Let's take a moment to explore why that phrase, which sounds like a concerned doctor giving genuine advice, can constitute as using rhetoric for harm. A 2017 article by the Cleveland Clinic explains how while C-sections are a modern technological marvel that helps save lives, they can be dangerous. One in three babies are born in the US via C-section, and this high number hints at an overuse of this surgical technique.[199]

The World Health Organization (WHO) recommends that C-section levels be between ten to fifteen percent at a maximum and only used when necessary. In a 2015 statement, the WHO states that "There is no evidence showing the benefits of caesarean delivery for women or infants who do not require the procedure. As with any surgery, caesarean sections are associated with short- and long-term risk which can extend many years beyond the current delivery and affect the health of the woman, her child, and future pregnancies. These risks are higher in women with limited access to comprehensive obstetric care."[200]

That means that while this surgical technique is certainly helpful for women who truly need the procedure due to labor

---

198 Marty Makary, *The Price We Pay*, 6.

199 Women's Health Team, "Why You Should Carefully Weigh C-Section Against a Vaginal Birth," *Health Essentials from Cleveland Clinic*, October 29, 2020.

200 AP Betran et al., "WHO Statement on Caesarean Section Rates," *BJOG: An International Journey on Obstetrics and Gynaecology* 123, no. 5 (July 22, 2015): 667-670.

complications, it should not be recommended by doctors without sufficient cause. However, a recent 2018 study found that C-section rates have been increasing rapidly around the world.[201] Of recent concern is the way this procedure creates "major microbial changes in the infant gut microbiome acquisition as a consequence of delivery mode and medical practices surrounding it." So, even though C-sections have been around from as early as the year 1500, we still don't understand the full short- and long-term effects of it on both mother and infant.[202]

So, now that we have some background information on C-sections, let's cycle back to Makary's comment. He describes how a certain OBGYN was known to unnecessarily nudge patients still in labor by the afternoon to get a C-section simply because the doctor wanted to get out of work early.[203] Knowing the risks of C-sections, hopefully it's clearer how this is an example of a doctor using rhetoric for harm. Here, the doctor is using rhetoric not to help the patient choose the labor path best for her and the baby (i.e., the lowest risk), he is using the power of persuasion to speed up the labor and birth process for his own benefit.

Unfortunately, doctors in different specialties have their own nudge words and phrases they use to intimidate patients into accepting certain treatments, particularly patients who don't

201 Silvia Arboleya et al., "C-Section and the Neonatal Gut Microbiome Acquisition: Consequences for Future Health," *Annals of Nutrition and Metabolism*, no. 73 (July 24, 2018): 17-23.

202 "Cesarean Section - A Brief History: Part 1," *U.S. National Library of Medicine*, National Institutes of Health, July 26, 2013.

203 Marty Makary, *The Price We Pay What Broke American Health Care - and How to Fix It*, 89.

have a medical background and aren't equipped with basic information about what a "normal" treatment looks like. As patients, we trust our doctors, and it's a shame that there are doctors who use rhetoric to harm and not help patients. "If an orthopedic surgeon is helping a patient decide between a knee replacement and a nonsurgical option, [the nudge phrase is] mentioning the joint is 'bone on bone,'" Makary wrote. "The phrase 'bone on bone' creates an image of grinding, like fingernails screeching on a chalkboard. Patients beg for it to stop. They choose surgery every time. And if a cardiologist tells a patient he has a 'widowmaker' in his heart—an actual medical term used to describe a partially blocked artery—the patient does whatever it takes to address it."[204]

Chances are, if you heard the phrase "widowmaker" associated with a bodily condition you have, your mind would immediately jump to thinking about how you can prolong your life to continue supporting your loved ones. Any proposed treatment after hearing that word, including a risky and unnecessary surgical treatment, would probably sound pretty appealing.

These are, unfortunately, only two examples of how some doctors rhetorically take advantage of their status as physicians, and the trust that we inherently give them, to unnecessarily operate on one of our most valuable possessions: our bodies. That said, I'm providing these examples not to encourage distrust in doctors; thankfully, most doctors are true to the Hippocratic oath. But, it's important for us to

---

204 Marty Makary, *The Price We Pay What Broke American Health Care - and How to Fix It*, 6.

understand how rhetoric is a double edged sword that can be used for evil, even by those whose job is to care for us.

Case study: Administration

Do you remember Vanessa Beasley, who introduced us to framing, lenses, and priming? During our interview, I was curious whether she, as someone who knows rhetorical techniques like the back of her hand, uses them at will. As we've seen, rhetoric can have infinite uses in our everyday lives, and I began to wonder whether there are situations where she purposely decides *not* to use her knowledge of rhetoric.

As an administrator in higher education, Beasley has to rely on rhetoric to succeed in her work. But there are instances when she decides it's not appropriate to use certain techniques. "Because I know what all the tricks are, I actually try to use the ones I think are ethical but also avoid the ones I think are not," Beasley said. "So, number one, I will never lie... If I don't know something I'll say I don't know it, I will never make a statement that is untrue. And that is partly because as we said...there is no filter for truth, so my position is if I'm going to be in a position as an administrator where I have a spotlight or where I have a microphone, then it's an ethical responsibility; I have to tell the truth."

To Beasley, it's unethical and hardly worth it when you lose peoples' trust. As we've learned, it's extremely important for leaders to maintain trust in order to manage people effectively. If they use rhetoric for harm, leaders risk losing that trust forever.

A 2019 *Harvard Business Review* article expressed a similar view, emphasizing the importance of "giving honest feedback" and consistency. "You must do what you say you will do," article authors Jack Zenger and Joseph Folkman wrote. "Follow through on your commitments and keep any promises you make."[205]

Even though leaders in organizations typically aren't directly held responsible for how they use rhetoric to communicate with others, consciously staying away from any tricky rhetoric that can even hint at dishonesty is something Beasley recommends. "I don't have to be voted in to have my job, but it does matter to me as an administrator, that students, faculty and staff trust me," Beasley said.

Case study: Politics

Earlier, we picked apart four different news articles covering the same topic: Judge Amy Coney Barrett's Senate confirmation hearings. Now, I want to turn to examining President Donald Trump's rhetoric more in-depth, as it caused quite a stir. Part of why his rhetoric is intriguing is how direct and unapologetic he is. In a field that is often mocked for being filled with lawyers tip toeing around certain words and issues, to many, Trump's rhetoric was a breath of fresh air.

Joshua Greene is a professor of Psychology at Harvard University, and was recently interviewed about "how Trump's rhetoric binds him to his tribe." Greene notes that unlike

---

205 "How Leaders Build Trust," *Harvard Business Review*, June 26, 2019.

most politicians that seek to widen their voter base with more moderate rhetoric, Trump relied on appealing to his most ardent supporters. Instead of trying to win moderates over and unite voters, Trump sought to isolate his supporters.[206]

For example, Trump accused President Obama of "treason" and called supporters of the Black Lives Matter movement (BLM) "terrorists." In contrast, most other politicians would likely say something like "I respect President Obama, but I think he's made some unethical choices recently," or "I strongly disagree with the Black Lives Matter movement." While these two revised, more rhetorically moderate phrases still get at the heart of what Trump wanted to convey (i.e., I think Obama is committing some suspicious acts against me, and the Black Lives Matter movement is frightening to me), they are much less accusatory and don't criminalize Obama or the BLM activists.

The difference between an unethical act and "treason" is historically poignant in the United States. The US was founded in part, to break away from monarchs who could accuse subjects of treason at will. So, accusing someone of "treason" in the US is unexpected and a bit extreme, as it implies that someone is opposing a king-like figure.

Although they are adept rhetoricians themselves who likely recognized the implications of Trump's rhetoric, many Senate Republicans refused to comment on Trump's accusation of "treason." Granted, some Republicans, including Senator

---

206 Joel Meares, "Q&A: Professor of Political Rhetoric Martin J. Medhurst," *Columbia Journalism Review*, January 10, 2011.

Thom Tillis and Senator Lindsey Graham, made clear that they didn't agree with the President. Others simply evaded the question and said, "I've got more important things to worry about."[207]

So why were some of Trump's fellow Republicans so hesitant to address his strongly accusatory rhetoric? Besides the fact that the claim was quite outlandish and made without any evidence, many Republicans knew that Trump's word choice was too extreme to defend. After all, he just accused Obama of trying to overthrow the government, according to Merriam-Webster's definition of "treason."[208]

Now, what about Trump's insistence that BLM supporters are "terrorists"? While there isn't a concrete agreed-upon political definition of what a "terrorist" is, Luis Schiumerini, an assistant professor of political science at the University of Notre Dame, pointed out that there is a pattern of politicians painting protestors in a negative light to steer focus away from the issue they're protesting about.

Schiumerini describes how instead of addressing protestors' specific concerns *about* the government, politicians in Iran, Hong Kong, and Turkey have tried to rebrand protestors as being *generally* anti-government. This often incites further divisiveness and unrest among citizens, letting the government off the hook. "Trying to brand protesters as terrorists, it's something we saw consistently in our study, especially in the case of Turkey," Schiumerini said. "For the government to

---

207 Andrew Desiderio and Marianne LeVine, "Republican Senators Refuse to Back Trump's 'Treason' Claim against Obama,"*Politico*, June 24, 2020.
208 *Merriam-Webster*, s.v. "treason (*n.*)," accessed February 22, 2021.

benefit from this, however, it's very important to turn public opinion to depict protesters in a negative fashion."[209]

We've broken down how Trump's rhetoric can suppress healthy discussion among his own party, and anger and unrest more generally. But a key question still remains: why did Trump choose to use the power of rhetoric in this way?

Rhetoric as a threat to democracy

As an experimental psychologist, Greene focuses on the scientific underpinnings of moral judgments and decision-making. To Greene, Trump's rhetoric is more than dangerous—it is threatening to destabilize democracy in the US. "What's new in the Trump era is not that both sides strongly prefer winning to losing," Greene said in an interview with *The Harvard Gazette*. "It's that the President himself is using systematic misinformation, the solicitation of foreign interference, threats of violence, and his power over government agencies (most notably the Postal Service) in order to disrupt the democratic process."

Trump intentionally used aggressive rhetoric filled with misinformation about facts, numbers, minority groups, and history to persuade his supporters that there is something terrible to fear. One infamous proclamation Trump made early on in his campaign to set an "us vs. them" tone was to paint all Mexicans as "drug dealers, criminals, [and]

---

209 Angela Dewan, "Trump Is Calling Protesters Terrorists. That Puts Him in the Company of the World's Autocrats," *CNN*, July 27, 2020.

rapists."[210] As we know from everyday life, no label applies to everyone who belongs to a certain group. Not all girls like pink and not all CEOs are men. Yet, Trump intentionally used rhetoric to cast certain groups of people as homogenous and unable to deviate from the norm.

So, what's the problem with using strong rhetoric to appeal to your side? Don't all politicians want to win? Greene describes how Trump's rhetoric, that proudly displays his sexist and racists views on his sleeve, is a clever strategy to bind his supporters even closer to him. This strategy of not only saying what others want to hear, but "proving" your view in an alienating way to non-supporters is referred to as "costly signaling." When you decide to get a twelve-inch bicep tattoo with your significant other's name, you're "proving" that you love them beyond words. And that's exactly the type of costly signaling Trump uses rhetorically. "He's not merely saying things that his supporters want to hear. By making himself permanently and unequivocally unacceptable to the opposition, he's 'proving' his loyalty to their side," Greene said. "This is why, I think, the Republican base trusts Trump like no other."

On the other hand, candidate Biden used rhetoric to try to appeal to as broad of a voter base as possible during his campaign. By using respectful, moderate rhetoric, and not calling Trump names in return, Biden did *not* alienate undecided moderates. But this means that he did not rally more extreme liberals either. So, by playing the divisive rhetorical

---

210 "'Drug Dealers, Criminals, Rapists': What Trump Thinks of Mexicans," *BBC News*, August 31, 2016.

card, Trump succeeded in increasing voter loyalty among his current base while simultaneously making more extreme liberals feel like Biden is a lukewarm supporter of their causes.

While some of you may be feeling both impressed and appalled by Trump's rhetorical tactics, I hope this brief analysis enlightens you of the dangers of rhetoric. Whether you agree with Trump's political views or not, his rhetoric has divided his own party by forcing people to either be with him or against him. It's also put a strain on Democrats, who feel pressured to respond to Trump's extreme signals by leaning more to the left to build a core group of extremely liberal supporters. Either way, most of us would agree that there's a better way to conduct politics, (i.e., without such toxic rhetoric).

Researchers at the University of California at Riverside conducted a study that showed how rhetoric that uses costly signals can encourage everyday people to lean into prejudices and assumptions.[211] This can also be dangerous because when misguided assumptions and beliefs are backed by governmental power, they can have detrimental effects on policy and citizens' everyday lives. Acting on unfounded assumptions is rarely a wise move.

In the study, 997 respondents were asked for their demographic information and political orientation. They were also asked how well "intelligent," "lazy," "violent," and "here legally" describe "most Hispanics in the United States." After gathering

---

211 Benjamin Newman et al., "Analysis | Trump's Rhetoric Does Encourage Open Prejudice and Bias. We Checked.," *The Washington Post*, March 11, 2020.

that preliminary information on respondents' biases, the researchers showed respondents one of five randomly assigned articles written by Democratic and Republican candidates on the subject. Finally, respondents were shown a short fictional excerpt describing how an employee named Darren did not like a new intern Miguel, and "regularly throws away Miguel's leftover food in the break room fridge, claiming that 'Miguel's food is greasy and smells up the fridge.'"

When asked to rank whether Daren's treatment of Miguel is socially acceptable or not, researchers found that respondents who read Trump's derogatory statements about Hispanics rated Daren's behavior as more socially acceptable. These respondents, who were already identified as "prejudiced" based on the survey they took before they read any statements, felt empowered by Trump's rhetoric to freely express their prejudice.

However, when respondents who were identified as "prejudiced" did not read Trump's statements, but other candidates', they scored Darren's treatment on the opposite spectrum, in the "unacceptable" range. These respondents' opinions on Hispanics in the US likely didn't change during the few minutes the study was conducted. So, what accounts for the differences in ratings for the two groups? Those who read Trump's rhetoric felt like it was acceptable to openly express their prejudiced viewpoints, while those who read other candidates' more moderate rhetoric were discouraged from applauding racially charged actions.

While we didn't go through each industry to examine how rhetoric can be used for harm, I wanted to briefly touch on a few examples that exemplify the dangers of rhetoric. So far, we've seen how rhetoric in advertising can encourage women to smoke (per our advertising discussion), increasing their likelihood of getting lung cancer by fifteen to thirty times than if they didn't smoke.[212] We've seen how rhetoric in medicine can discourage patients from getting the help they need, or drive them to "choose" riskier and costlier treatments they *don't* need. And we've seen how rhetoric in politics can encourage deep divisions and civil unrest.

What I want you to takeaway is this: rhetoric is a tool that can be used to achieve tremendous success, but it's like playing with fire. If you're careless with it, or worse yet, intentionally use it for harm, you'll end up hurting those around you. And, you may end up creating consequences that come back to bite you.

Throughout this book, we've learned how to build a rhetorical toolkit that's ready to help you take control of any situation. We've also discussed practical exercises you can incorporate into your everyday life that will help you use language to positively impact others and accomplish your goals. Armed with the tools and strategies from this book, you're ready to take your communication and persuasive skills to the next level. But, I hope you will view the conclusion of this book as not the end, but the beginning of a lifelong journey to become a master rhetorician.

It seems fitting to close with a thought from Aristotle, the scholar we started our rhetorical journey with, on how we

---

212 "What Are the Risk Factors for Lung Cancer?," *Centers for Disease Control and Prevention*, September 22, 2020.

should properly use rhetoric in our everyday lives. In *The Art of Rhetoric,* he states:

"Whatever creates or increases happiness or some part of happiness, we ought to do; whatever destroys or hampers happiness, or gives rise to its opposite, we ought not to do." [213]

213 Aristotle, *The Art of Rhetoric,* Translation and Index by W. Rhys Roberts (Megaphone eBooks, 2008), 25.

Acknowledgements

Writing this book has been a long, challenging, and exciting journey. I'm thrilled that it's finally here, and that you've finished it! So, thank you, reader, for joining me on this journey. Thanks to Eric Koester for the opportunity and Brian Bies for the publishing assistance. Writing this book involved many individuals generously devoting their time to helping this project succeed. I'd like to thank all of my interviewees, in particular Marvin Diogenes for his guidance and mentorship in tackling this complex discipline to which he has devoted his career to teaching. A big thank you to Hemma Lomax and Tom Lee for their continued mentorship as well.

I'd like to also thank my family and friends for their support and enthusiasm for this project. Many thanks to Katherine Mazoyer and Elizabeth Covington for their edits and suggestions, as well as my wonderful beta readers (Marie, Jessica, Eric, Griffin, and Drake) for their thoughtful feedback. You all helped push me as a writer and take this book to the next level.

In addition, I want to thank everyone who pre-ordered my book. I'm still heart-warmed by your outpouring of support, generosity, and interest. This book couldn't have made it from laptop to page without you! Many thanks to you all (listed in category and order of support):

Author Champions: Tsung-I Huang, Philip Hsu, Wen Chong Huang, Juliana Shay

Supporters: Eric Suh, Raymond Hsu, Tony Huang, Susan Wang, Calvin Huang, Grace Chou, and Wilson Chu

Paperback supporters: Griffin Patterson, Lulu Duan, Veer Shah, Shannon Yan, Michael He, Lucas Martim de Lima Portilho, Angel Asirvatham, Elaine Wu, Victoria Lising, MarieFaith Lane, Cristian Ochoa, Olivia Arnold, Andrew Xu, Charis Ling, Josephine Hartmann, Rohit Kataria, Jessica Mo, Alexandra Blumenfled, Annabelle McNeill, Joanna McInnes, Claire Chen, Shravya Vasireddy, Emily Goncalves, Eric Koester, Ava Dziadzio, Tewen Hsu, Miquéla Thornton, Gigi Belay, Jennifer Greenman, Chia-Chien Chang, Samuel Zhu, Fang Long Wei, Andrea, Kong, Jerry Lee, Yuanyuan Lee, Allison Carter, Grace Yang, Annika Quam, Alex Tang, Jillian Gonzales, Joanna Shih, Tina Smith, Neo Scott, Andy Ruan, Anne-Marie Steppling, Daniel Williams, Abby Wei, Eva Starr, Jake Haskins, Sophie Vogelsang, Daniel Song, Emma Willey, Jadyn Rogers, Davi Lennon, Angelina Guhl, Ao Qu, Joanne Chen, Jinwen Chen, Liam Hall, Amisha Mittal, Braeden Abrahamsen, and Hogan Sherrow

Ebook supporters: Alex Cuc, Drake White, Dennis Chen, Darwin Ma, Matt Zhang, Bing Chen, Julianna Darby, Deborah Sheng, Helmut Konz, Rio Jia, Brianna Stewart, Grace Lamont, Ruth Chen, Grant Kinsey, Mark Raj, Josh Miller,

Chase Mandell, Thomas Hum, Claudia Cornelison, Yamei Usui, Michelle Liu, Joseph Qiu, Kate Kim, Heather Mewkill, Hannon Eberts, Edward Xiao, Marty Grady, Katie Cella, Eva Herr, Benjamin Shapiro, Hitha Uday, Kate Schaller, Wesley Viera, Ellie Hooey, Jason Platkin, Jeff Huang, Annabelle Li, Erin McConnell, Angela Wu, Ching-Song Wei, Jong Eun Jung, Kelsey Zhu, Sophia Chen, Nia Dorsey, Cynthia Sheng, Miranda Deng, Srish Kumar, Robert McCarthy, Claire Rich, Shruti Anat, Sophia Clark, Jackie Rhoads, Monica Liu, Yanni Zhang, Paige Clancy, Samantha Schneid, Wen-Chian Wei, Yi-Chen Lee, Cameron Madden, Sarah Landry, Ashley Kim, Sofia Oliveres, Alice Qiao, Lu Cao, Sophia She, Riddhi Singhania, Helen Qian, Jordan DeTar, Caroline Lee, Nicholas Toy, Deborah Park, Sung Jin Lee, Dylan Katz, Sarah Bellete, Kelsey Donohue, Zak Stengel, Jenna Wang, Karman Nagra, Noah Frank, Young Kim, Bharath Nagarajan, Jack Bowen, Luke Kobrin, Joy Zhang, Stella Wang, Kate Petosa, Kevin Loo, Shun Ahmed, Tariah Lane, Jack Mok, Carson Ferrara, Wesley Jung, Madison Woods, and Kathryn Lee

Appendix

___

Introduction

Cohen, Patricia. "A Rising Call to Promote STEM Education and Cut Liberal Arts Funding." *The New York Times*, February 21, 2016. https://www.nytimes.com/2016/02/22/business/a-rising-call-to-promote-stem-education-and-cut-liberal-arts-funding.html.

Deming, David. "In the Salary Race, Engineers Sprint but English Majors Endure." *The New York Times*, September 20, 2019. https://www.nytimes.com/2019/09/20/business/liberal-arts-stem-salaries.html.

Handelsman, Jo and Megan Smith. "STEM for All." National Archives and Records Administration, February 11, 2016. https://obamawhitehouse.archives.gov/blog/2016/02/11/stem-all.

Kessler, Glenn and Joe Fox. "Analysis | The False Claims That Trump Keeps Repeating." *The Washington Post*, November 6, 2020. https://www.washingtonpost.com/graphics/politics/

fact-checker-most-repeated-disinformation/?tid=graph-ics-story.

Merriam-Webster. s.v. "app (n.)." Accessed April 6, 2016._https://
www.merriam-webster.com/dictionary/rhetoric_ (https://
www.merriam-webster.com/dictionary/rhetoric).

Ossola, Alexandra. "Is the U.S. Focusing Too Much on STEM?"
The Atlantic, December 3, 2014. https://www.theatlantic.com/
education/archive/2014/12/is-the-us-focusing-too-much-on-
stem/383353/.

Chapter 1

Encyclopaedia Britannica Online. Academic ed. s.v. "Rhetoric."
Accessed November 1, 2020._https://www.britannica.com/
topic/rhetoric#ref29023_ (https://www.britannica.com/topic/
rhetoric#ref29023).

Merriam-Webster. s.v. "app (n.)." Accessed April 6, 2016._https://
www.merriam-webster.com/dictionary/rhetoric_ (https://
www.merriam-webster.com/dictionary/rhetoric).

Rapp, Christof. "Aristotle's Rhetoric." Stanford Encyclopedia of
Philosophy. Stanford University, February 1, 2010. https://plato.
stanford.edu/entries/aristotle-rhetoric/#4.3.

TED. "Camille Langston: How to use rhetoric to get what you
want." September, 2016. Video, 2:35. https://www.ted.com/talks/
camille_langston_how_to_use_rhetoric_to_get_what_you_
want/transcript#t-158010_.

TED. "Camille Langston: How to use rhetoric to get what you want." September, 2016. Video, 3:32. https://www.ted.com/talks/camille_langston_how_to_use_rhetoric_to_get_what_you_want/transcript#t-158010_.

TED. "Camille Langston: How to use rhetoric to get what you want." September, 2016. Video, 1:51. https://www.ted.com/talks/camille_langston_how_to_use_rhetoric_to_get_what_you_want/transcript#t-158010_.

Chapter 2

Cicero. "De Inventione ." *Loeb Classical Library*, n.d. https://www.loebclassics.com/view/marcus_tullius_cicero-de_inventione/1949/pb_LCL386.23.xml?readMode=recto.

Lumen Learning. "Principles of Public Speaking." The Roman Republic's Adoption of Rhetoric Principles of Public Speaking. Accessed November 1, 2020. https://courses.lumenlearning.com/suny-publicspeakingprinciples/chapter/the-roman-republics-adoption-of-rhetoric/#return-footnote-415-2.

Martin Lowther Clarke. "Quintilian." Encyclopædia Britannica. Last updated January 1, 2021. https://www.britannica.com/biography/Quintilian.

Quintilian. "Institutio Oratoria (Book 2)." Quintilian, Institutio Oratoria, Book 2, chapter 16. Accessed February 10, 2021. http://www.perseus.tufts.edu/hopper/text?doc=Perseus%3Atext%3A2007.01.0060%3Abook%3D2%3Achapter%3D16.

University of Arkansas Sam M. Walton College of Business. "The
Five Canons of Rhetoric." Accessed November 1, 2020. https://
walton.uark.edu/business-communication-lab/Resources/
downloads/The_Five_Canons_of_Rhetoric.pdf.

Chapter 3

Brummett, Barry. Rhetoric in popular culture. *Sage Publications*,
2017.

"Cultural Rhetoric." Stanford Undergrad. Accessed February 10, 2021.
https://undergrad.stanford.edu/pwr-track/cultural-rhetoric.

Shuter, Robert. The Cultures of Rhetoric. *International and Intercultural Communication Annual* 22, (1999): 11-18.

Chapter 4

Anonymous. Bob Woodward, n.d. https://www.bobwoodward.
com/.

Anonymous. "Amy Coney Barrett: Trump US Supreme Court Pick
Grilled on Presidential Powers." *BBC News*. October 15, 2020.
https://www.bbc.com/news/world-us-canada-54536803.

Biskupic, Joan. "Amy Coney Barrett's Answers Were Murky but
Her Conservative Philosophy Is Clear." *CNN*. Cable News Network, October 15, 2020. https://www.cnn.com/2020/10/15/pol-
itics/amy-coney-barrett-conservative-philosophy/index.html.

D'Alessio, Dave and Mike Allen. "Media Bias in Presidential Elections: A Meta-Analysis," *Journal of Communication* 50, no. 4 (December 2000): 133–156. https://doi-org.proxy.library.vanderbilt.edu/10.1111/j.1460-2466.2000.tb02866.x.

Elving, Ron. "What Happened With Merrick Garland In 2016 And Why It Matters Now." *NPR*, June 29, 2018. https://www.npr.org/2018/06/29/624467256/what-happened-with-merrick-garland-in-2016-and-why-it-matters-now.

Gramlich, John. "Q&A: How Pew Research Center Evaluated Americans' Trust in 30 News Sources." *Pew Research Center.* January 24, 2020. https://www.pewresearch.org/fact-tank/2020/01/24/qa-how-pew-research-center-evaluated-americans-trust-in-30-news-sources/.

History.com Editors, History.com Editors. "Watergate Scandal." *History.com*. A&E Television Networks. Last updated September 25, 2019. https://www.history.com/topics/1970s/watergate.

LeVine, Marianne. "McConnell Fends off Accusations of Hypocrisy over Holding Supreme Court Vote." *POLITICO*. September 22, 2020. https://www.politico.com/news/2020/09/21/mcconnell-pushes-back-hypocrisy-supreme-court-419569.

Schultz, Marisa. "Judge Amy Coney Barrett Flips the Script on Democrats over Health Care, Notes When She Adopted Daughter." *Fox News*. FOX News Network, October 13, 2020. https://www.foxnews.com/politics/judge-amy-coney-democrats-health-care-adoption.

Schwartz, John and Hiroko Tabuchi. "By Calling Climate Change 'Controversial,' Barrett Created Controversy." *The New York Times*. Updated October 22, 2020. https://www.nytimes.com/2020/10/15/climate/amy-coney-barrett-climate-change.html.

Starkey, Guy. Balance and Bias in Journalism: Representation, Regulation and Democracy. Basingstoke: Palgrave Macmillan, 2007.

Tran, Delbert. "The Fourth Estate As The Final Check." Yale Law School. Media Freedom and Information Access Clinic, November 22, 2016. https://law.yale.edu/mfia/case-disclosed/fourth-estate-final-check.

Woodward, Bob. "Guiding Principles" in "Bob Woodward Teaches Investigative Journalism." November 13, 2020. MasterClass video, 4:08. https://www.masterclass.com/classes/bob-woodward-teaches-investigative-journalism/chapters/guiding-principles.

Woodward, Bob. "Guiding Principles" in "Bob Woodward Teaches Investigative Journalism." November 13, 2020. MasterClass video, 5:55. https://www.masterclass.com/classes/bob-woodward-teaches-investigative-journalism/chapters/guiding-principles.

Woodward, Bob. "Students Dig Into Woodward's Interview With Trump" in "Bob Woodward Teaches Investigative Journalism." November 13, 2020. MasterClass video, 2:09. https://www.masterclass.com/classes/bob-woodward-teaches-investigative-journalism/chapters/students-dig-into-woodward-s-interview-with-trump.

Chapter 5

Anonymous. "Understanding the Epidemic." Centers for Disease Control and Prevention. March 19, 2020. https://www.cdc.gov/drugoverdose/epidemic/index.html.

Anonymous. "'Right to Die'," Cornell Law School Legal Information Institute. https://www.law.cornell.edu/constitution-conan/amendment-14/section-1/right-to-die.

Anonymous. "Martin Adel Makary, M.D., M.P.H., Professor of Surgery." Johns Hopkins Medicine. https://www.hopkinsmedicine.org/profiles/results/directory/profile/0018306/martin-makary.

Harford, Tim. "US Healthcare Is Literally Killing People." *Financial Times*. July 12, 2019. https://www.ft.com/content/05f7fa82-a315-11e9-a282-2df48f366f7d.

Holt, Terrence. "With Pandemic Information Overload How Can We Tell What Is Real?" *Literary Hub*, August 4, 2020. https://lithub.com/with-pandemic-information-overload-how-can-we-tell-what-is-real/.

Kabisch, Maria, et al. "Randomized controlled trials: part 17 of a series on evaluation of scientific publications." *Dtsch Arztebl Int*. 108, no. 39 (Sep 2011):663-668. doi:10.3238/arztebl.2011.0663.

Khazan, Olga. "The 3 Reasons the U.S. Health-Care System Is the Worst." *The Atlantic*. June 22, 2018. https://www.theatlantic.com/health/archive/2018/06/the-3-reasons-the-us-healthcare-system-is-the-worst/563519/.

Macy, Beth. Dopesick: Dealers, Doctors, and the Company That Addicted America. Boston: Little, Brown and Company, 2018.

Makary, Marty. The Price We Pay What Broke American Health Care - and How to Fix It. New York: Bloomsbury Publishing, 2019.

Murphy, Brendan. "How Humanities Background Could Make You a Better Medical Student." *American Medical Association.* March 5, 2020. https://www.ama-assn.org/residents-students/ preparing-medical-school/how-humanities-background- could-make-you-better-medical.

Ratzan, Richard M., "How to Fix the Premedical Curriculum— Another Try." *JAMA* 322, no. 8 (August 27, 2019): 710–711. https://doi:10.1001/jama.2019.11480

Warren, Kenneth S. "The Humanities in Medical Education." *Annals of Internal Medicine* 101, no. 5 (November 1, 1984): 697– 701. https://doi.org/https://doi.org/10.7326/0003-4819-101-5-697.

Williams, Mia. "Addiction: Is It a Disease or a Choice?" *Addiction Center*, December 7, 2017. https://www.addictioncenter.com/ community/addiction-is-it-a-disease-or-a-choice/.

Yong, Ed. "Immunology Is Where Intuition Goes to Die." *The Atlantic.* August 5, 2020. https://www.theatlantic.com/health/ archive/2020/08/covid-19-immunity-is-the-pandemics- central-mystery/614956/.

Chapter 6

Adams, Tim. "How Freud Got under Our Skin." *The Guardian*. March 10, 2002. https://www.theguardian.com/education/2002/mar/10/medicalscience.highereducation.

Anonymous. "Consumer Culture [5W PR 2020 Report] - NY PR Agency 5W Public Relations Blog." 5W Public Relations, February 20, 2020. https://www.5wpr.com/new/research/5wpr-2020-consumer-culture-report/.

Anonymous. "We Belong to Something Beautiful." Sephora. https://www.sephora.com/beauty/belong.

Anonymous. "The Rise of American Consumerism." *PBS*. Public Broadcasting Service. https://www.pbs.org/wgbh/americanexperience/features/tupperware-consumer/.

Encyclopaedia Britannica Online. Academic ed. s.v. "Psychoanalytic Theory." Accessed January 15, 2021. https://www.britannica.com/biography/Sigmund-Freud/Psychoanalytic-theory#ref1250116.

Anonymous, "Woodrow Wilson," The White House (The United States Government), accessed January 15, 2021, https://www.whitehouse.gov/about-the-white-house/presidents/woodrow-wilson/#:~:text=Woodrow%20Wilson%2C%20a%20leader%20of,the%20world%20safe%20for%20democracy.%E2%80%9D.

Anonymous. "The Story of Propaganda: AHA." American Historical Association. Accessed January 15, 2021. https://www.historians.org/about-aha-and-membership/aha-history-

and-archives/gi-roundtable-series/pamphlets/em-2-what-is-propaganda-(1944)/the-story-of-propaganda.

Curtin, Melanie. "73 Percent of Millennials Are Willing to Spend More Money on This 1 Type of Product." *Inc.com*. March 30, 2018. https://www.inc.com/melanie-curtin/73-percent-of-millennials-are-willing-to-spend-more-money-on-this-1-type-of-product.html.

Curtus, Adam. "The Century of Self," Youtube video (Documentary).

Donnelly, Christopher, and Renato Scaff. "Who Are the Millennial Shoppers? And What Do They Really Want?"

Accenture. *Outlook: The journal of high-performance business,* August 13, 2020. https://www.accenture.com/us-en/insight-outlook-who-are-millennial-shoppers-what-do-they-really-want-retail.

Guttmann, A. "Advertising Market Worldwide - Statistics & Facts." *Statista*, January 15, 2021. https://www.statista.com/topics/990/global-advertising-market/.

Goodby, Jeff & Rich Silverstein. "Working With Brands" in "Jeff Goodby & Rich Silverstein Teach Advertising and Creativity." November 13, 2020. MasterClass video, 0:48. https://www.masterclass.com/classes/jeff-goodby-and-rich-silverstein-teach-advertising-and-creativity/chapters/working-with-brands.

Goodby, Jeff & Rich Silverstein. "On Craft: Writing, Design, and Giving Direction," in "Jeff Goodby & Rich Silverstein Teach

Advertising and Creativity." November 13, 2020. MasterClass video, 6.28. https://www.masterclass.com/classes/jeff-goodby-and-rich-silverstein-teach-advertising-and-creativity/chapters/on-craft-writing-design-and-giving-direction

Goodby, Jeff & Rich Silverstein. "It's Great, but They'll Never Buy It: Selling a Crazy Idea," in "Jeff Goodby & Rich Silverstein Teach Advertising and Creativity." November 13, 2020. MasterClass video, 5:20. https://www.masterclass.com/classes/jeff-goodby-and-rich-silverstein-teach-advertising-and-creativity/chapters/it-s-great-but-they-ll-never-buy-it-selling-a-crazy-idea.

Goodby, Jeff & Rich Silverstein. "Advertising Is Everything… and Everything Is Advertising," in "Jeff Goodby & Rich Silverstein Teach Advertising and Creativity." November 13, 2020. MasterClass video, 7:54. https://www.masterclass.com/classes/jeff-goodby-and-rich-silverstein-teach-advertising-and-creativity/chapters/advertising-is-everything-and-everything-is-advertising.

Hanbury, Mary. "Meet the Startup Founder Challenging the Way Women Shop for Bras." *Business Insider,* April 18, 2019. https://www.businessinsider.com/thirdlove-changing-bra-shopping-online-2019-4#:~:text=ThirdLove%20is%20built%20around%20being%20body%2Dinclusive&text=In%20its%20most%20recent%20campaign,size%20in%20the%20same%20style.

Haselton, Todd. "How to Find out What Google Knows about You and Limit the Data It Collects." *CNBC,* December 6, 2017. https://www.cnbc.com/2017/11/20/what-does-google-know-about-me.html#:~:text=It%20collects%20data%20on%20what,it%20thinks%20you'll%20like.

History.com Editors. "Paris Peace Accords Signed." *History.com.* A&E Television Networks, last updated May 12, 2020. https://www.history.com/this-day-in-history/paris-peace-accords-signed.

Johnson, Kai. "How Values-Driven Social Campaigns Help Businesses Make an Impact - Salesforce Blog." *Salesforce.*

Salesforce, May 5, 2020. https://www.salesforce.com/blog/2020/05/values-driven-marketing-social-campaigns.html.

Taylor, Victoria. "Victoria's Secret's 'Perfect Body' Ads Draw Criticism." *nydailynews.com*, October 29, 2014. https://www.nydailynews.com/life-style/victoria-secret-perfect-body-ads-draw-criticism-article-1.1992023.

Wong, Curtis M. "Axe's New 'Find Your Magic' Ad Promotes A Different Type Of Masculinity." *HuffPost*, January 14, 2016. https://www.huffpost.com/entry/axe-commercial-vogue-queens_n_5697cf66e4b0778f46f85fc2.

Chapter 7

Agarwal, Dr. Pragya. "Here Is How Unconscious Bias Holds Women Back." *Forbes Magazine*, December 17, 2018. https://www.forbes.com/sites/pragyaagarwaleurope/2018/12/17/here-is-how-unconscious-bias-holds-women-back/#14d4f6052d4f.

Anonymous. "Robert A. Iger." The Walt Disney Company. Accessed February 3, 2021. https://thewaltdisneycompany.com/leaders/robert-a-iger/.

Anonymous. "Hannah Riley Bowles," Women and Public Policy Program, Harvard Kennedy School, accessed February 4, 2021. https://wappp.hks.harvard.edu/people/hannah-riley-bowles.

Bowles, Hannah Riley. "Claiming Authority: How Women Explain their Ascent to Top Business Leadership Positions." Research in Organizational Behavior 32 (2012): 189–212.

Cain, Áine, Hollis Johnson, and Sarah Jacobs. "Free, Unlimited Snacks Are Becoming a Common Office Perk - Here's How Companies like Facebook and LinkedIn Feed Their Employees." *Business Insider*, December 8, 2016. https://www.businessinsider.com/food-facebook-linkedin-uber-yelp-kickstarter-2016-12#there-are-also-plenty-of-snack-bars-dotted-throughout-the-office-7.

Cassidy, Anne. "Clocking off: the Companies Introducing Nap Time to the Workplace." *The Guardian*. December 4, 2017. https://www.theguardian.com/business-to-business/2017/dec/04/clocking-off-the-companies-introducing-nap-time-to-the-workplace.

Chin, Stacey, Alexis Krivkovich, and Marie-Claude Nadeau. "Closing the Gap: Leadership Perspectives on Promoting Women in Financial Services." *McKinsey & Company*September 6, 2018. https://www.mckinsey.com/industries/financial-services/our-insights/closing-the-gap-leadership-perspectives-on-promoting-women-in-financial-services.

Cotter, David A., Joan M. Hermsen, Seth Ovadia, Reeve Vanneman, "The Glass Ceiling Effect," *Social Forces* 80, no. 2 (December 2001): 655–681, https://doi.org/10.1353/sof.2001.0091.

Heilman, M. E., & Caleo, S. "Gender discrimination in the workplace." *Oxford library of psychology*, (2018): 73–88.

Harris, Chelsea A et al. "What is in a Pronoun?: Why Gender-fair Language Matters." *Annals of surgery 266*, no.6 (2017): 932-933. doi:10.1097/SLA.0000000000002505.

Iger, Bob. "Tenets for Success" in "Bob Iger Teaches Business Strategy and Leadership." November 13, 2020. MasterClass video, 7:59. https://www.masterclass.com/classes/bob-iger-teaches-business-strategy-and-leadership/chapters/tenets-for-success.

Iger, Bob. "The Art of Negotiation" in "Bob Iger Teaches Business Strategy and Leadership." November 13, 2020. MasterClass video, 3:39. https://www.masterclass.com/classes/bob-iger-teaches-business-strategy-and-leadership/chapters/tenets-for-success.

Iger, Bob. "Focus, Strategy, and Priorities" in "Bob Iger Teaches Business Strategy and Leadership." November 13, 2020. MasterClass video, 4:10. https://www.masterclass.com/classes/bob-iger-teaches-business-strategy-and-leadership/chapters/focus-strategy-priorities.

Iger, Bob. "Creating Brand Value" in "Bob Iger Teaches Business Strategy and Leadership." November 13, 2020. MasterClass video, 5:27. https://www.masterclass.com/classes/bob-iger-teaches-business-strategy-and-leadership/chapters/creating-brand-value.

Lotze, Kristen. "10 Tech Companies with Generous Parental Leave Benefits." *TechRepublic*, February 15, 2019. https://www.techrepublic.com/article/10-tech-companies-with-generous-parental-leave-benefits/.

Navarrete, Carlos David, Andreas Olsson, Arnold K. Ho, Wendy Berry Mendes, Lotte Thomsen, and James Sidanius. "Fear Extinction to an Out-Group Face: The Role of Target Gender." *Psychological Science* 20, no. 2 (February 2009): 155–58. https://doi.org/10.1111/j.1467-9280.2009.02273.x.

Sullivan, John. "How Google Reinvented HR and Drives Success through People Analytics." *Inside HR*, November 27, 2013. https://www.insidehr.com.au/how-google-reinvented-hr/.

Chapter 8

Anonymous. "Section 4: Demographics and Political Views of News Audiences." *Pew Research Center - U.S. Politics & Policy*. Pew Research Center, September 27, 2012. https://www.pewresearch.org/politics/2012/09/27/section-4-demographics-and-political-views-of-news-audiences/.

Anonymous. "3. Views of the Economic System and Social Safety Net." *Pew Research Center - U.S. Politics & Policy*. Pew Research Center, December 17, 2019. https://www.pewresearch.org/politics/2019/12/17/views-of-the-economic-system-and-social-safety-net/.

Anonymous. "Martin Medhurst." Department of Political Science | Baylor University. Accessed January 20, 2021. https://www.baylor.edu/political_science/index.php?id=956222.

Anonymous. "P.R. Chari." The Brookings Institution. Accessed February 14, 2021. https://www.brookings.edu/author/p-r-chari/.

Anonymous. "Remarks by Deputy Chief of Mission Michael Newbill at the Combating Fake News Conference." U.S. Embassy in Cambodia, October 29, 2018. https://kh.usembassy.gov/remarks-by-deputy-chief-of-mission-michael-newbill-at-the-combating-fake-news-conference/.

AP. "The Gorbachev Visit; Excerpts From Speech to U.N. on Major Soviet Military Cuts." The New York Times, December 8, 1988. https://www.nytimes.com/1988/12/08/world/the-gorbachev-visit-excerpts-from-speech-to-un-on-major-soviet-military-cuts.html.

Biser, Margaret. "The Fireside Chats: Roosevelt's Radio Talks." The White House Historical Association, August 19, 2019.https://www.whitehousehistory.org/the-fireside-chats-roosevelts-radio-talks.

Cournoyer, Caroline. "Trump Promised to Eliminate the National Debt. It Has Risen by $3 Trillion." CBS News. CBS Interactive, October 29, 2019. https://www.cbsnews.com/news/trump-promised-to-eliminate-the-national-debt-it-has-risen-by-3-trillion/.

Cunningham, Sean. "A Short History of Presidential Communication." InsideHook, June 14, 2018. https://www.insidehook.com/article/history/short-history-presidential-communication.

Chari , P. R., and Michael Newbill. "Declaratory Diplomacy: Rhetorical Initiative and Confidence Building." Stimson Center,

September 14, 1999. https://www.stimson.org/1999/declaratory-diplomacy-rhetorical-initiative-and-confidence-building/.

DeVega, Chauncey. "Ralph Nader on Trump's Corruption, 'Corporate State Fascism' and Why Democrats Keep Losing." *Salon.* Salon.com, October 26, 2020. https://www.salon.com/2020/10/26/ralph-naders-election-wisdom-in-the-swing-states-you-have-to-vote-for-joe-biden/.

Earll, Carrie Gordon. "Abortion and ObamaCare." Focus on the Family, January 1, 2014. https://www.focusonthefamily.com/pro-life/abortion-and-obamacare/.

Ekins, Emily. "What Americans Think About Poverty, Wealth, and Work." Cato Institute, September 24, 2019. https://www.cato.org/publications/survey-reports/what-americans-think-about-poverty-wealth-work#null.

"Reagan Recovers in Second Debate, Oct. 21, 1984." *POLITICO,* October 21, 2018. https://www.politico.com/story/2018/10/21/this-day-in-politics-oct-21-1984-910774.

History.com Editors. "Jimmy Carter." *History.com.* A&E Television Networks, November 12, 2019. https://www.history.com/topics/us-presidents/jimmy-carter.

History.com Editors. "The Kennedy-Nixon Debates." *History.com.* A&E Television Networks, September 21, 2010. https://www.history.com/topics/us-presidents/kennedy-nixon-debates.

Howard, Jenny. "Plague Was One of History's Deadliest Diseases-Then We Found a Cure." *National Geographic,* July 6, 2020.

https://www.nationalgeographic.com/science/health-and-human-body/human-diseases/the-plague/#:~:text=The%20plague%20killed%20an%20estimated,in%20which%2070%2C000%20residents%20died.

Kelly, Caroline. "HHS Unveils New Requirement for Abortion Coverage Payments under Obamacare." *CNN.* Cable News Network, December 20, 2019. https://www.cnn.com/2019/12/20/politics/hhs-abortion-premium-payment-obamacare/index.html.

Kennedy, John F. "Commencement Address at American University, Washington, D.C., June 10, 1963." Commencement Address at American University, Washington, D.C., June 10, 1963 | JFK Library. Accessed February 14, 2021. https://www.jfklibrary.org/archives/other-resources/john-f-kennedy-speeches/american-university-19630610.

Larrabee, F. Stephen. "Gorbachev and the Soviet Military." Foreign Affairs 66, no. 5 (1988): 1002-026. Accessed February 15, 2021. doi:10.2307/20043575.

Lipton, Eric. "'The Coal Industry Is Back,' Trump Proclaimed. It Wasn't." *The New York Times,* October 5, 2020. https://www.nytimes.com/2020/10/05/us/politics/trump-coal-industry.html.

Madhani, Aamer. "As Crime Surges on His Watch, Trump Warns of Biden's America." *AP NEWS.* Associated Press, July 29, 2020. https://apnews.com/article/ap-top-news-politics-joe-biden-lifestyle-election-2020-344477113461be394548f8ce775313dc.

Mayer, Jane. "Donald Trump's Ghostwriter Tells All." *The New Yorker*. July 18, 2016. https://www.newyorker.com/magazine/2016/07/25/donald-trumps-ghostwriter-tells-all.

"What Athenian Democracy Can Teach Us." *The Philosophical Salon*, July 16, 2020. http://thephilosophicalsalon.com/what-athenian-democracy-can-teach-us/?mc_cid=438594e213&mc_eid=4cobdcfd1d.

"Q&A: Professor of Political Rhetoric Martin J. Medhurst." *Columbia Journalism Review*, January 10, 2011. https://archives.cjr.org/campaign_desk/qa_professor_of_political_rhet.php.

Mineo, Liz. "Harvard Expert Compares 1918 Flu, COVID-19." *Harvard Gazette*, July 21, 2020. https://news.harvard.edu/gazette/story/2020/05/harvard-expert-compares-1918-flu-covid-19/.

Morgan, Robin. "Persuasion: The Debates: Robin Morgan: Author, Activist, Feminist: NYC." Robin Morgan, September 27, 2020. https://www.robinmorgan.net/blog/persuasion-the-debates/.

"P.R. Chari." Brookings. Accessed February 22, 2021. https://www.brookings.edu/author/p-r-chari/.

Pehar, Drazen. "Historical Rhetoric and Diplomacy - An Uneasy Cohabitation." Historical rhetoric and diplomacy - An uneasy cohabitation | DiploFoundation. Accessed February 14, 2021. https://www.diplomacy.edu/resources/general/historical-rhetoric-and-diplomacy-uneasy-cohabitation.

Shamekh, A., Mahmoodpoor, A., & Sanaie, S. "COVID-19: Is it the black death of the 21st century?" *Health promotion perspectives* 10, no. 3 (2020): 166–167. https://doi.org/10.34172/ hpp.2020.27.

Thompson, Derek. "Busting the Myth of 'Welfare Makes People Lazy'." *The Atlantic*. March 8, 2018. https://www.theatlantic. com/business/archive/2018/03/welfare-childhood/555119/.

Encyclopaedia Britannica Online. Academic ed. s.v. "Walter Mondale." Last updated January 1, 2021. https://www.britannica. com/biography/Walter-Mondale.

Encyclopaedia Britannica Online. Academic ed. s.v. "United States Presidential Election of 1984." October 30, 2020. https:// www.britannica.com/event/United-States-presidential-election-of-1984.

Encyclopaedia Britannica Online. Academic ed. s.v. "Appeasement." Accessed February 14, 2021. https://www.britannica. com/topic/appeasement-foreign-policy.

Encyclopaedia Britannica Online. Academic ed. s.v.. "Killed, Wounded, and Missing." Accessed February 14, 2021. https:// www.britannica.com/event/World-War-I/Killed-wounded-and-missing.

Encyclopaedia Britannica Online. Academic ed. s.v. "Ralph Nader." February 23, 2020. https://www.britannica.com/biography/ Ralph-Nader.

"Why Diplomacy Matters - United States Department of State." U.S. Department of State, U.S. Department of State, April 17, 2019, www.state.gov/remarks-at-texas-am-wiley-lecture-series/

(http://www.state.gov/remarks-at-texas-am-wiley-lecture-series/) (http://www.state.gov/remarks-at-texas-am-wiley-lecture-series/ (archived).

Chapter 9

Abramson, Leigh McMullan. "Is There a Career in Law That Doesn't Lead to Burnout?" *The Atlantic*. September 10, 2015. https://www.theatlantic.com/business/archive/2015/09/work-life-balance-law/404530/#:~:text=At%20many%20large%20firms%2C%20lawyers,actually%20working%2060%20to%2070.

Anonymous. "Memory Lapse or Dementia? 5 Clues to Help Tell the Difference." Johns Hopkins Medicine. Accessed January 27, 2021. https://www.hopkinsmedicine.org/health/wellness-and-prevention/memory-lapse-or-dementia-5-clues-to-help-tell-the-difference.

Anonymous. "History of Court Dress." Courts and Tribunals Judiciary. Accessed January 27, 2021. https://www.judiciary.uk/about-the-judiciary/the-justice-system/history/.

DeMers, Jayson. "10 Presentation Tricks to Keep Your Audience Awake." *Inc.com*. Inc., August 11, 2015. https://www.inc.com/jayson-demers/10-presentation-tricks-to-keep-your-audience-awake.html.

Gorman, Carol Kinsey. "5 Ways Body Language Impacts Leadership Results." Forbes. August 26, 2018. https://www.forbes.com/sites/carolkinseygoman/2018/08/26/5-ways-body-language-impacts-leadership-results/?sh=4b9f124d536a.

Gregoire, Carolyn. "The Fascinating Science Behind 'Talking' With Your Hands." *HuffPost*, February 4, 2016. https://www. huffpost.com/entry/talking-with-hands-gestures_n_56afc-faae4b0b8d7c230414e#:~:text=Hand%20gestures%20help%20 us%20take,and%20use%20more%20declarative%20lan-guage.%E2%80%9D

North, Marjorie. "10 Tips for Improving Your Public Speaking Skills." Harvard Division of Continuing Education Blogs, March 17, 2020. https://blog.dce.harvard.edu/professional-de-velopment/10-tips-improving-your-public-speaking-skills.

White, James Boyd - University of Michigan Law School. Accessed February 22, 2021. https://www.law.umich.edu/FacultyBio/Pages/FacultyBio.aspx?FacID=jbwhite.

White, James Boyd. "Law as Rhetoric, Rhetoric as Law: The Arts of Cultural and Communal Life." *The University of Chicago Law Review* 52, no. 3 (1985): 684-702. Accessed February 20, 2021. doi:10.2307/1599632.

Chapter 10

Anonymous. "Measles Cases and Outbreaks." Centers for Disease Control and Prevention. Centers for Disease Control and Pre-vention, December 2, 2020. https://www.cdc.gov/measles/cas-es-outbreaks.html.

Anonymous. "Proposal Writing." Northwestern University Office of Undergraduate Research. Accessed January 28, 2021. https://undergradresearch.northwestern.edu/advising/proposal-writing/.

Anonymous. "Home." Home - Neil deGrasse Tyson. Accessed January 28, 2021. https://www.haydenplanetarium.org/tyson/.

Barnette, Adrian, and Danielle Herbert. "The Personal Cost of Applying for Research Grants." *The Guardian*. April 7, 2014. https://www.theguardian.com/higher-education-network/blog/2014/apr/07/applying-research-grant-stressful-university.

"Best Colleges with Technical and Scientific Communication Degrees." Universities.com. Accessed February 22, 2021. https://www.universities.com/programs/technical-and-scientific-communication-degrees.

Boulanger, Amy. "Anti Vaxxers: Understanding Opposition to Vaccines." *Healthline*. Healthline Media, September 15, 2017. https://www.healthline.com/health/vaccinations/opposition#results.

Collins, H.M., and Robert Evans. "The Third Wave of Science Studies: Studies of Expertise and Experience." *Social Studies of Science* 32, no. 2 (April 2002): 235–96. https://doi.org/10.1177/0306312702032002003.

Dignen, Bob. "Five Reasons Why Feedback May Be the Most Important Skill." *Cambridge University Press*, March 17, 2014. https://www.cambridge.org/elt/blog/2014/03/17/five-reasons-feedback-may-important-skill/.

Epstein, David. *Range: How Generalists Triumph in a Specialized World*. (Macmillian, 2020).

Gigante, Maria E. "Critical Science Literacy for Science Majors: Introducing Future Scientists to the Communicative Arts." *Bulletin of Science, Technology & Society* 34, no. 3–4 (June 2014): 77–86. https://doi.org/10.1177/0270467614556090.

Green, Bill. "There's No Such Thing as a Stupid Question. Here's How You Can Empower Your Employees to Ask for Help." *Inc. com.* Inc., March 19, 2019. https://www.inc.com/bill-green/ theres-no-such-thing-as-a-stupid-question-heres-how-you- can-empower-your-employees-to-ask-for-help.html.

Hales, Andrew H, and Kipling D Williams. "Alienating the Audi- ence: How Abbreviations Hamper Scientific Communication." *Association for Psychological Science*, January 31, 2017. https:// www.psychologicalscience.org/observer/alienating-the-audi- ence-how-abbreviations-hamper-scientific-communication.

Herbert, Danielle L. et al., "On the Time Spent Preparing Grant Proposals: an Observational Study of Australian Researchers," *BMJ Journals*, British Medical Journal Publishing Group, no. 3 (2013). http://dx.doi.org/10.1136/bmjopen-2013-002800.

James, Geoffrey. "You Simply Won't Believe How Much Time You Waste in Meetings at Work, According to MIT." *Inc.com.* Inc., September 23, 2019. https://www.inc.com/geoffrey-james/you- simply-wont-believe-how-much-time-you-waste-in-meetings- at-work-according-to-mit.html.

Kennedy, Brian, and Meg Hefferon. "What Americans Know About Science." *Pew Research Center Science & Society.* Pew Research Center, May 28, 2019. https://www.pewresearch.org/ science/2019/03/28/what-americans-know-about-science/.

Pace, Michael L et al., "Communicating with the Public: Opportunities and Rewards for Individual Ecologists," *The Ecological Society of America* 8, no. 6 (August 1, 2010), https://doi.org/ https://doi.org/10.1890/090168.

Rogelberg, Steven G, Cliff W Scott, and John Kello . "The Science and Fiction of Meetings." *MIT Sloan Management Review* 48, no. 2 (December 2007).

Rull, Valentí. "The most important application of science: As scientists have to justify research funding with potential social benefits, they may well add education to the list." *EMBO reports* no. 15 (2014): 919-22. doi:10.15252/embr.201438848.

"Science Communication and Outreach Careers." University of California San Francisco: Office of Career and Professional Development. Accessed February 22, 2021. https://career. ucsf.edu/phds/non-academic/every-month/science-communication.

"Science Communication in United States: 49,350 Results." LinkedIn, February 22, 2021. https://www.linkedin.com/jobs/science-communication-jobs/.

Sohn, Emily. "Secrets to Writing a Winning Grant." *Nature News*. December 20, 2019. https://www.nature.com/articles/d41586-019-03914-5.

Tyson, deGrasse Neil. Neil deGrasse Tyson Teaches Scientific Thinking and Communication. MasterClass, November 13, 2020.

Chapter 11

Alter, Rebecca. "A Guide to Every Writers' Room on Late-Night TV." *Vulture*, March 20, 2020. https://www.vulture.com/article/late-night-writers-guide.html.

Anonymous. "Hans Zimmer." *IMDb*. IMDb.com. Accessed January 31, 2021. https://www.imdb.com/name/nm0001877/bio?ref_=nm_ov_bio_sm.

Anonymous. "Giving Thanks Can Make You Happier." *Harvard Health*, https://www.health.harvard.edu/healthbeat/giving-thanks-can-make-you-happier#:~:text=Gratitude%20is%20a%20thankful%20appreciation,receives%2C%20whether%20tangible%20or%20intangible.&text=Gratitude%20helps%20people%20feel%20more,express%20gratitude%20in%20multiple%20ways.

Anonymous. "Joyce E.A. Russell." *The Washington Post*. WP Company. Accessed January 31, 2021. https://www.washingtonpost.com/people/joyce-ea-russell/.

Hansen, Liane, and David Folkenflik. "The Power of the 24-Hour News Cycle." *NPR*, May 29, 2005. https://www.npr.org/templates/story/story.php?storyId=4671485.

Koblin, John. "Stephen Colbert Signs a New 'Late Show' Deal Through 2023." *The New York Times*, October 17, 2019. https://www.nytimes.com/2019/10/17/business/media/stephen-colbert-late-show-cbs.html.

Otterson, Joe. "'Late Show With Stephen Colbert' Narrowly Tops Late-Night Ratings for 2018-2019 Season." *Variety*, May 22, 2019. https://variety.com/2019/tv/news/late-show-with-stephen-colbert-ratings-2018-2019-1203223520/.

Pringle, Patricia. "Clearing the Air - the Power of Apology in Japan." Japan Intercultural Consulting, July 18, 2020. https://japanintercultural.com/free-resources/articles/clearing-the-air-the-power-of-apology-in-japan/.

Roberts, Robin. "Meet Your Instructor," in "Robin Roberts Teaches Effective and Authentic Communication." October 1, 2020. MasterClass video, 3:07. https://www.masterclass.com/classes/robin-roberts-teaches-effective-and-authentic-communication/chapters/meet-your-instructor.

Roberts, Robin. "Public Speaking," in "Robin Roberts Teaches Effective and Authentic Communication." October 1, 2020. MasterClass video, 1:17. https://www.masterclass.com/classes/robin-roberts-teaches-effective-and-authentic-communication/chapters/public-speaking.

Roberts, Robin. "Behind-the-Scenes at Good Morning America," in "Robin Roberts Teaches Effective and Authentic Communication." October 1, 2020. MasterClass video, 5:12. https://www.masterclass.com/classes/robin-roberts-teaches-effective-and-authentic-communication/chapters/behind-the-scenes-at-good-morning-america.

Russell, Joyce E.A. "Career Coach: The Power of an Apology." *The Washington Post*. September 25, 2011. https://www.washingtonpost.com/business/capitalbusiness/career-coach-the-power-of-an-apology/2011/09/21/gIQAANkqwK_story.html.

Sarkis, Stephanie. "Apologizing Is A Strength, Not A Weakness." *Forbes Magazine*, September 29, 2019. https://www.forbes.com/sites/stephaniesarkis/2019/09/29/apologizing-is-a-strength-not-a-weakness/#1db714714061.

Zimmer, Hans. "Directors: Part 2" in "Hans Zimmer Teaches Film Scoring". January 21, 2021, MasterClass video, 2:13.https://www.masterclass.com/classes/hans-zimmer-teaches-film-scoring/chapters/directors-part-2.

Zimmer, Hans. "Directors: Part 1" in "Hans Zimmer Teaches Film Scoring". January 21, 2021, MasterClass video, 1:51. https://www.masterclass.com/classes/hans-zimmer-teaches-film-scoring/chapters/directors-part-1.

Chapter 12

Cheney, George, Lars Thøger Christensen, Charles Conrad, and Daniel J. Lair. "Corporate Rhetoric as Organizational Discourse." *The SAGE Handbook of Organizational Discourse*, (2004): 79-104. http://dx.doi.org/10.4135/9781848608122.n4.

Goodby, Jeff & Rich Silverstein, "On Craft: Writing, Design, and Giving Direction," in "Jeff Goodby & Rich Silverstein Teach Advertising and Creativity." November 13, 2020. MasterClass video, 7:16. https://www.masterclass.com/classes/jeff-goodby-and-rich-silverstein-teach-advertising-and-creativity/chapters/on-craft-writing-design-and-giving-direction.

Rogelberg, Steven G, and Liana Kreamer . "The Case for More Silence in Meetings." *Harvard Business Review*, June 14, 2019. https://hbr.org/2019/06/the-case-for-more-silence-in-meetings.

Rogers, Kristie. "Do Your Employees Feel Respected?" *Harvard Business Review*, June 21, 2018. https://hbr.org/2018/07/do-your-employees-feel-respected.

Chapter 13

Acharya, S., & Shukla, S. (2012). Mirror neurons: Enigma of the metaphysical modular brain. *Journal of natural science, biology, and medicine*, 3(2), 118–124. https://doi.org/10.4103/0976-9668.101878.

Black, Matthew P., Athanasios Katsamanis, Brian R. Baucom, Chi-Chun Lee, Adam C. Lammert, Andrew Christensen, Panayiotis G. Georgiou, and Shrikanth S. Narayanan. "Toward Automating a Human Behavioral Coding System for Married Couples' Interactions Using Speech Acoustic Features." *Speech Communication*. North-Holland, December 16, 2011. https://www.sciencedirect.com/science/article/pii/S0167639311001762.

Bowles, Hannah Riley, and Bobbi Thomason. "Negotiating Your Next Job." *Harvard Business Review*, December 15, 2020. https://hbr.org/2021/01/negotiating-your-next-job.

Gyurak, A., Gross, J. J., & Etkin, A. (2011). "Explicit and implicit emotion regulation: a dual-process framework." *Cognition & emotion,* 25(3), 400–412. https://doi.org/10.1080/02699931.2010.544160.

Hilaire, Chris St, and Lynette Padwa. *27 Powers of Persuasion: Simple Strategies to Seduce Audiences & Win Allies*. New York: Prentice Hall Press, 2011.

James, Geoffrey. "You Simply Won't Believe How Much Time You Waste in Meetings at Work, According to MIT." *Inc.com*, Inc., 23 Sept. 2019, www.inc.com/geoffrey-james/you-simply-wont-believe-how-much-time-you-waste-in-meetings-at-work-according-to-mit.html.

"Partisan Antipathy: More Intense, More Personal." *Pew Research Center - U.S. Politics & Policy*, Pew Research Center, 17 Aug. 2020, www.pewresearch.org/politics/2019/10/10/partisan-antipathy-more-intense-more-personal/?utm_source=link_newsv9.

PON Staff. "Essential Negotiation Skills: Limiting Cognitive Bias in Negotiation: Essential Business Negotiation Strategies and Tactics to Create Value at the Bargaining Table." Harvard Law School, program on negotiation, January 21, 2021. https://www.pon.harvard.edu/daily/negotiation-skills-daily/integrative-negotiation-and-negotiating-rationally/.

Nauert, Rick. "Tone of Voice Trumps Word Choice in Spousal Arguments." Psych Central, 8 Aug. 2018, psychcentral.com/news/2015/11/24/tone-of-voice-more-important-than-word-choice-during-spousal-arguments/95304.html.

Voss, Christopher, and Tahl Raz. *Never Split the Difference: Negotiating as If Your Life Depended on It*. London: RH Business Books, 2016.

Voss, Chris. "Mirroring," in "Chris Voss Teaches The Art of Negotiation." November 13, 2020. MasterClass video, 6:54. https://www.masterclass.com/classes/chris-voss-teaches-the-art-of-negotiation/chapters/mirroring.

Voss, Chris. "Labeling," in "Chris Voss Teaches The Art of Negotiation." November 13, 2020. MasterClass video, 4:22. https://www.masterclass.com/classes/chris-voss-teaches-the-art-of-negotiation/chapters/labeling.

Voss, Chris. "The Accusations Audit," in "Chris Voss Teaches The Art of Negotiation." November 13, 2020. MasterClass video, 1:56. https://www.masterclass.com/classes/chris-voss-teaches-the-art-of-negotiation/chapters/the-accusations-audit.

Shearer, Jeffrey Gottfried and Elisa. "News Use Across Social Media Platforms 2016." Pew Research Center's Journalism Project, 27 Aug. 2020, www.journalism.org/2016/05/26/news-use-across-social-media-platforms-2016/.

The Black Swan Group. "Chris Voss." Black Swan. Accessed February 4, 2021. https://www.blackswanltd.com/our-team/chris-voss.

The Science and Fiction of Meetings. *MIT Sloan Management Review*, 2007.

Torre, Jared B., and Matthew D. Lieberman. "Putting Feelings Into Words: Affect Labeling as Implicit Emotion Regulation." *Emotion Review* 10, no. 2 (April 2018): 116–24. https://doi.org/10.1177/1754073917742706.

Whitbourne, Susan Krauss. "In-Groups, Out-Groups, and the Psychology of Crowds." Psychology Today, Sussex Publishers, 7 Dec. 2010, www.psychologytoday.com/us/blog/fulfillment-any-age/201012/in-groups-out-groups-and-the-psychology-crowds.

Chapter 14

"About MHFA." Mental Health First Aid, February 16, 2021. https://www.mentalhealthfirstaid.org/about/.

"Arthur Kleinman." Anthropology Department. Accessed February 20, 2021. https://anthropology.fas.harvard.edu/people/arthur-kleinman.

Awaysheh, Abdullah et al. "A review of medical terminology standards and structured reporting." *Journal of veterinary diagnostic investigation,* 30, no. 1 (2018): 17-25. doi:10.1177/1040638717738276.

Berkenkotter, Carol. *Patient Tales: Case Histories and the Uses of Narrative in Psychiatry.* Columbia: University of South Carolina Press, 2008.

"Center for Student Wellbeing." Vanderbilt University. Accessed February 20, 2021. https://www.vanderbilt.edu/healthydores/.

Corrigan, P. W., & Watson, A. C. "Understanding the impact of stigma on people with mental illness." *World psychiatry* 1, no. 1 (2002): 16–20.

"Friendship and Mental Health." *Mental Health Foundation,* August 14, 2018. https://www.mentalhealth.org.uk/a-to-z/f/ friendship-and-mental-health.

Kleinman, Arthur. *The Illness Narratives: Suffering, Healing, and the Human Condition.* New York: Basic Books, 1988.

"Mental Illness." National Institute of Mental Health. U.S. Department of Health and Human Services, January 2021. https://www.nimh.nih.gov/health/statistics/mental-illness.shtml.

Mental Health First Aid USA. "The Quiet Power of Empathic Listening." *Mental Health First Aid,* July 28, 2017. https://www.mentalhealthfirstaid.org/2017/07/quiet-power-listening/.

Molloy, Cathryn. "Recuperative ethos and agile epistemologies: Toward a vernacular engagement with mental illness ontologies." *Rhetoric Society Quarterly* 45, no. 2 (2015): 138-163.

Chapter 15

Arboleya, Silvia, M. Suárez, N. Fernández, L. Mantecón, G. Solís, M. Gueimonde, and C.G. de los Reyes-Gavilán. "C-Section and the Neonatal Gut Microbiome Acquisition: Consequences for Future Health." Annals of Nutrition and Metabolism. Karger Publishers, July 24, 2018. https://www.karger.com/Article/Abstract/490843.

Betran, AP, MR Torloni, JJ Zhang, and AM Gülmezoglu. "WHO Statement on Caesarean Section Rates." *BJOG: An International Journal of Obstetrics and Gynaecology,* July 22, 2015.

https://obgyn.onlinelibrary.wiley.com/doi/full/10.1111/1471-0528.13526.

"Cesarean Section - A Brief History: Part 1." U.S. National Library of Medicine. National Institutes of Health, July 26, 2013. https://www.nlm.nih.gov/exhibition/cesarean/part1.html#:~:text=Perhaps%20the%20first%20written%20orecord,unable%20to%20deliver%20her%20baby.

"Greek Medicine - The Hippocratic Oath." U.S. National Library of Medicine. National Institutes of Health, February 7, 2012. https://www.nlm.nih.gov/hmd/greek/greek_oath.html.

"How Leaders Build Trust." *Harvard Business Review*, June 26, 2019. https://hbr.org/tip/2019/06/how-leaders-build-trust.

Desiderio, Andrew, and Marianne LeVine. "Republican Senators Refuse to Back Trump's 'Treason' Claim against Obama." *POLITICO*, June 24, 2020. https://www.politico.com/news/2020/06/23/republican-senate-trump-treason-obama-336097. Angela Dewan, "Trump Is Calling Protesters Terrorists. That Puts Him in the Company of the World's Autocrats," CNN, July 27, 2020.

Dewan, Angela. "Trump Is Calling Protesters Terrorists. That Puts Him in the Company of the World's Autocrats." *CNN*. Cable News Network, July 27, 2020. https://www.cnn.com/2020/07/25/politics/us-protests-trump-terrorists-intl/index.html.

"'Drug Dealers, Criminals, Rapists': What Trump Thinks of Mexicans." *BBC News*. BBC, August 31, 2016. https://www.bbc.com/news/av/world-us-canada-37230916.

MacBride, Elizabeth. "Stereotyping Makes People More Likely to Act Badly." Stanford Graduate School of Business, June 5, 2015. https://www.gsb.stanford.edu/insights/stereotyping-makes-people-more-likely-act-badly.

Meares, Joel. "Q&A: Professor of Political Rhetoric Martin J. Medhurst." *Columbia Journalism Review*, January 10, 2011. https://archives.cjr.org/campaign_desk/qa_professor_of_political_rhet.php.

Newman, Benjamin, Jennifer Merolla, Loren Collingwood, and Karthick Ramakrishnan. "Analysis | Trump's Rhetoric Does Encourage Open Prejudice and Bias. We Checked." *The Washington Post*. March 11, 2020. https://www.washingtonpost.com/politics/2020/03/11/trumps-rhetoric-does-encourage-open-prejudice-bias-we-checked/.

"What Are the Risk Factors for Lung Cancer?" Centers for Disease Control and Prevention, September 22, 2020. https://www.cdc.gov/cancer/lung/basic_info/risk_factors.htm#:~:text=People%20who%20smoke%20cigarettes%20are,the%20risk%20of%20lung%20cancer.

Women's Health Team. "Why You Should Carefully Weigh C-Section Against a Vaginal Birth." Health Essentials from Cleveland Clinic, October 29, 2020. https://health.clevelandclinic.org/why-you-should-carefully-weigh-c-section-against-a-vaginal-birth/.

9 781636 768304